THE
DIVERTING HISTORY
OF A
LOYALIST TOWN

The
DIVERTING HISTORY
of a
LOYALIST TOWN

A Portrait of St. Andrews, New Brunswick

by

Grace Helen Mowat

BRUNSWICK PRESS - *Publishers*
FREDERICTON, NEW BRUNSWICK, CANADA

COPYRIGHT, CANADA
1953
by BRUNSWICK PRESS, LIMITED
All Rights Reserved
ISBN 0 88790 009 7

FIRST EDITION 1932
SECOND EDITION 1953
THIRD EDITION 1976

PRINTED IN CANADA
by UNIVERSITY PRESS of NEW BRUNSWICK, LIMITED
FREDERICTON, NEW BRUNSWICK, CANADA

CONTENTS

FOREWORD

FOREWORD

The story of St. Andrews is unique in the history of Canada, and it is most fitting that Miss Grace Helen Mowat's fascinating records of the early days should be kept in print.

An earlier edition of *The DIVERTING HISTORY of a LOYALIST TOWN* has for many years been unobtainable outside the libraries and private homes of those who obtained copies more than twenty years ago.

Miss Mowat adds a chapter to her book which brings the history up to date and she is to be complimented on her lucidity of expression as well as the freshness of her memory.

Miss Mowat is an authority on the traditions of Charlotte County and scarcely a week goes by but the Registry Office sends on to her a visitor who has called to inquire about his ancestry. Miss Mowat is tireless in her activities on behalf of these strangers. In her new edition Miss Mowat tells us the disposition of the famous homes and houses of early St. Andrews, as well as adding an excellent account of those who have within the last few years built summer houses or year-round residences in the charming seaboard town.

D. L. MacLaren, P.C.,
Lieutenant-Governor of New Brunswick.

THE LOYALIST

Wild war and discord once combined
    And rolled their deadly thunder,
And here beyond the Western Main
    Our Empire rent asunder.

I then forsook my native home
    Where long I'd been a lodger,
And in New Brunswick joined my fate
    With many a toil-worn soldier.

And in the wide extending woods
    I fixed my habitation,
Content to claim the British name
    Through life in every station.

I chose to rank myself among
    The subjects of our nation—
To brave each want connected with
    My forlorn situation.

Grim winter's fierce protracted reign
    Most grievously oppressed me.
Lank hunger raised his pinching hand
    And sorely he distressed me.

My children called aloud for bread—
    Alas! I'd none to give them.
I ranged the woods, I scooped the flood,
    For something to relieve them.

Hard-hearted want at length retired
    And smiling plenty hailed me;
I tilled the ground which proved a source
    Of wealth that never failed me.

9

Snug in my cot, grim winter's reign
No longer now oppressed me;
Lank hunger raised his arm in vain,
No longer he distressed me.

I've lived to see New Brunswick boast
A hardy population;
Excelled, in no respect, by those
Of any State or nation.

Her commerce circling far and wide,
Her force and power increasing,
Her soil supplying nations' wants,
A source of wealth unceasing.

O Liberty! thou goddess bright,
By mortals fondly courted,
I left thy blazoned name behind
Still by thyself supported.

Thou heavenly form! in rustic garb
I freely still embrace thee;
No tyrants here, or slaves are seen,
To banish or disgrace me.

Long live the King! may peace and health
Through many years attend him,
And from the bitter ills of life
May Heaven still defend him.

The above poem was found in manuscript among some old papers; the authorship is unknown.

1 FRENCH PERIOD

THE old Loyalist Town, that I tell you of, lies hidden from the bay of Fundy by countless islands, that shelter the peaceful waters of Passamaquoddy Bay. There it lies, stretching its length of sandstone shores peacefully in the sunshine, a tranquil little seaport, surrounded by hills and sea, resting in the afterglow of a romantic past and the peaceful leisure of an uncommercial present.

The Indians call this place Qua-nos-cumcook. This name looks formidable, written down, but it is clear music when an Indian says it. Sentimental tourists now call it "St.-Andrews by-the-Sea" without ever asking permission at the town office. But the Frenchman, who placed the St. Andrews cross there far back in the dim ages, called it St. Andrews, so the Indians said, and St. Andrews it has been ever since, and that is its name—St. Andrews, Shiretown of the County of Charlotte, in the Province of New Brunswick—by the Grace of God—possessing a court house, a jail, a town hall and five churches. What more is required in an old Loyalist Town? Only the romantic past, that I mentioned before, which is to be the subject of this history.

To begin at the beginning—the very beginning; a glacier—enormous, powerful, slow moving—came down straight from Baffin Land with a pocketful of little islands. At least, that is what a scientist told me, (and who can contradict a scientist?) On came the glacier, dragging everything before it. It took five hundred feet, or so, off the top of Chamcook mountain to add to its collection. And when it came to the water, it left the bay dotted with little islands, hundreds of them, all shapes and sizes, and there they have remained ever since.

Now, it was a pleasant gesture of the glacier to place all those little islands as it did; they make it nice for everybody. For the Indians who catch their seals and porpoise there; for the fishermen, to set their weirs and lobster traps; for the farmers, to pasture their sheep, and for tourists and pleasure seekers, for picnics and sailing parties; and so, many thanks to the glacier.

After the glacier came the Indians, a peaceable tribe of Micmacs. They had their headquarters at Joe's Point and camped about, wherever the game was plentiful. Then one eventful day they saw what they thought were strange looking birds coming to them across the waters. But they were not birds, but white-sailed ships such as they had never seen before. So did the white man come to the waters of Quoddy.

We don't know how many years the French and English traded with the Indians before they settled down to found a colony, but in the year 1604 Champlain came sailing across the bay, and up the wide mouth of the river and landed on a little island that, by mistake, had dropped out of the glacier's pocket when it was wrestling with the top of Chamcook. On that Island was founded the first settlement of the white man in Acadia. They called both the island and the river St. Croix, because when sailing up the river they found it had three branches that formed a somewhat irregular cross.

With Champlain came a distinguished band of French gentlemen: Marc Lescarbot, the poet and historian, Sieur DeMonts and Jean Biencour, Pontgravé and Poutrincourt, Champdore and D'Orville; besides these were artisans, farmers, priests, Huguenots, soldiers, merchanics and adventurers, all anxious to settle the New World and claim it for France, or at least as much of it as they could. They were a courageous little company and well equipped too, with all kinds of tools and building material, garden seeds and ammunition.

They set themselves merrily to work through the pleasant summer and autumn. No place could be more delightful. They set up their cannon on the little island at the southern extremity that connected with the main island at low tide. Much of this tiny island fortress has been washed away since; indeed, the outlines of the whole island were much larger in Champlain's day than they are now.

At the northern end of the island they built dwelling places and forts, a chapel and a gallery, wherein to exercise on stormy days.

Then Poutrincourt sailed back to France, promising to send them supplies in the spring. He left them one barque and one small boat. There they were for the winter, the only white settlement in all that vast wilderness. And little they knew about the winter that was ahead of them.

And the winter came upon them suddenly and unexpectedly. Nothing in their sunny France had prepared them for its piercing cold or the severity of its wild snow storms. They realized then that they had chosen their place of settlement unwisely. Their first thought had been its advantages of fortification from attacks by the Indians.

In the graceful words of that most charming person, Marc Lescarbot, the island had: "three special discommodities: want of wood (for that which was in the said isle, was spent in buildings); lack of fresh water, and the continued watch made by night, fearing some surprise from the savages that had lodged themselves at the foot of the said island, or some other enemy.

"When they had need of water or wood, they were constrained to cross over the river, which is twice as broad as the Seine. It was a thing painful and tedious in such sort that it was needful to keep the boat a whole day before one might get those necessaries."

In addition to these "discommodities" it was impossible to keep their supplies from freezing; even their wine froze, so we are told. Worse still, an unknown sickness came upon them, probably scurvy, and many of their number died and the others were so prostrated it was difficult to care for the sick or bury the dead.

Marc Lescarbot thus describes it:

"For remedies there was none to be found. The poor sick creatures did languish, pining away by little and little for want of sweet meats, as milk or spoon meats for to sustain their stomachs, which could not sustain the hard meats by reason of let, proceeding from a rotten flesh, which grew and overbounded within their mouthes."

The coming of spring and warmer weather brought relief to the sufferers, but the little colony was sadly wasted and disheartened. Of the seventy-nine who had remained on the island, thirty-five had died during the winter. DeMonts decided to remove the colony to Port Royal.

Pontgravé, returning from France, brought them fresh supplies and forty men, and assisted the distressed colony to move their possessions across the bay. The buildings that had been raised with so much hope and energy were abandoned and the Indians were left again in sole possession of the land.

Very little is known about this region for many years after that. We hear vague tales of traders and fishermen frequenting the Islands of Passamaquoddy. The Frenchmen, too, returned occasionally, for Lescarbot tells us that they had planted rye on the St. Croix Island, but left before it had matured; but that two years after, they returned to find that it had increased wonderfully so that "they did gather of it as fair, big and weighty as any in France".

Of the Frenchman who placed the St. Andrews cross at the mouth of the river and said a prayer for the blessing of the land, we know only from Indian tradition, but the name St. Andrews was used for some time before the coming of the Loyalists.

15

The same Frenchman, so the Indians say, placed another cross at Point Migic, at the mouth of the Magaguadavic River, and this in after years led to much trouble and confusion as to which river was the real St. Croix.

2   THE LOYALISTS

E NGLISH traders came to the shores of Passama-quoddy about the year 1760, and some attempt at settlement on the islands seems to have been made a few years later.

In 1770, William Owen obtained a grant of the Island of Campobello, which soon developed into a considerable settlement. There the Owen family remained for over a century, living like feudal lords, entertaining with lavish hospitality and governing their possession with kindly, but despotic authority.

Deer Island about this time came into the possession of another English gentleman, Captain Farrell, and a social life developed among the Islands, but on the mainland there was little or no settlement till the year 1783. Islands in those days were more accessible when boats were the chief means of transportation.

Then came the Loyalists, and with their coming the town of St. Andrews was founded.

The great majority of the Loyalists who were exiled from the States at the close of the Revolutionary War, embarked from New York, where they had assembled under the military protection of Sir Guy Carleton. Poor Sir Guy, we are told, was completely snowed under with Loyalists, who swarmed his garrison; and nobly he grappled with their problems, finding ships for their transportation and provisions for their maintenance, lands for them to dwell in and balm for their lacerated feelings. An extract from an old letter written from New York at this period is of interest. The letter* is headed "On Board the *Tryal, off Staten Island, Nov. 29th, 1783*", and is written to Edward Winslow, then in Nova Scotia arranging for the settlement of the Loyalists; the writer is his friend Ward Chipman, afterwards one of the prominent founders of Saint John. He writes:

"I have been a witness to the mortifying scene of giving up the city of New York to the American troops. About 12 o'clock on Tuesday, the 25th inst., all our troops were paraded on the wide ground before the Provost, where they remained till the Americans, about 1 o'clock, marched in through Queen Street and Wall Street and the Broad-way, when they wheeled off to the hay-wharf and embarked immediately and fell down to Staten Island. I walked out and saw the American troops, under General Knox, march in, and was one of the last on shore in the city; it really occasioned most painful sensation and I thought Sir Guy Carleton, who was on parade, looked unusually dejected. The particular account of the business of the day you will find in the newspaper which I have enclosed to Blowers. I have passed two days since,

---

* Published in the Winslow papers.

in the city to which I returned upon finding all was peace and quiet; a more shabby, ungentlemanlike-looking crew than the new inhabitants are, I never saw, tho' I met with no insult or molestation. The Council for sixty days, which is invested with supreme authority for that term, is sitting. What will be determined by them is uncertain; many are apprehensive of violent and severe measures against individuals. I paid my respects to Generals Knox and Jackson, the latter is Commandant of the city; they received me very politely. I had the satisfaction also of seeing General Washington, who is really a good-looking, genteel fellow. Scarce any of our friends, or any man of respectability, remains at New York."

The New York Loyalists were sent in great numbers to Saint John, which was then a part of the Province of Nova Scotia and under the jurisdiction of Halifax; it was at the time called Parrtown. They were supplied by the government with boards, nails and window glass, tools of various kinds and, for those going farther up the river, a cow and a plow. All disbanded soldiers received an axe and a spade and their half pay. Rations of food and clothing were distributed among them and continued to be doled out in gradually lessening quantities for three years. The government supplies were not always on hand when required and families who had settled farther up the river were difficult to reach during the winter, and many hardships were endured during the first winter. In those days of slow transportation it was a considerable undertaking for any Government to supply thirty thousand refugees, suddenly transplanted from comfortable, often luxurious, homes, with sufficient supplies to keep them in the mere necessities of life in that country that was then little more than a wilderness.

We often hear the comment in these later days, by those who are unfamiliar with the true history of the Loyalists, that they were foolish to have left the "good land of the free". Why could they not have stayed in their comfortable homes and been contented with a President, instead of fleeing to the lands governed by an obnoxious King? The Loyalists unfortunately, or perhaps fortunately, had no alternative; their property was destroyed, their lands confiscated, they were ill-treated at every turn and in some instances put to death, and finally proscribed and banished.

American history has little to say on this subject; it is naturally more impressed by British tyranny. British history is equally silent. The rebellion in the American colonies meant little to historians busy recording French conflicts and the Napoleonic wars. The vision of a united Empire, its value to trade and commerce as seen by the more widely travelled and better educated colonists, were invisible to the advocates of "liberty, fraternity and equality".

That the Colonists had grievances, the Loyalists did not deny. They had grievances themselves when they formed their own colonies, but they overcame them without rebellions. The treaty of 1783 had provided that their property would be respected, and it is probable that Washington and all those possessed with wisdom and authority would have gladly prevented the persecution of the Loyalists, but in that wide and scattered country it was impossible to restrain the

19

excited and victorious rabble that inevitably follows in the trail of all revolution. They longed to give a practical demonstration of their new found "liberty, fraternity and equality". They construed "liberty" into plunder, and "equality" into insulting those to whom they had once been subordinate, with the derisive cry of "Tory".

So it was that thirty thousand perfectly good, honest British subjects packed up their worldly goods in brass-studded "hair trunks", and with their family plate, family portraits and old mahogany, sailed off in ship loads to the Bay of Fundy.

If the story of the Loyalists is inadequately told in history, it has been often told and retold by the firesides of remote country homes—told to the children for bedtime stories—told at Christmas festivities and anniversaries, when whole families came to spend the day. Still they are told, even unto this day—stories of suffering, banishment and privation, courage, endurance and resourceful reconstruction.

You will find the story also silently folded up in bundles of old yellow letters stowed away in those same old hair trunks that the Loyalists brought.

It is all a very strange romantic story when you piece it together bit by bit. The story of an exiled people, landing with their traditions of refinement, their priceless heirlooms, their children and servants, in a land that they must reclaim from the forest. And after all, it was lovely land and they soon learned to love it. Where could there be found a more fitting setting for a tale of romance?

3   FOR KING AND COUNTRY

IN READING over letters of this interesting period, we find ourselves modifying our attitude towards George III. We are so accustomed to hearing of him as the "cruel tyrant" of the American school book, and just as frequently English historians will represent him as the "stubborn monarch" who lost the Colonies for Britain. He was always the unfortunate peg on which both sides hung the responsibilities of the revolution. Poor simple-minded old King, with his supercilious ministers and his profligate sons. He was deeply touched by the tales from over the sea of loyal subjects who would sacrifice all for king and country. His kind heart grieved for their sufferings. His only tyranny was to insist that their persecutors be disciplined. Can he be blamed for that, when tales came back from overseas that these loyal subjects were robbed, insulted, thrown into filthy prisons, even at times used as slaves—tales of wanton destruction of property that were hailed as heroic patriotism? How could those rebels expect representation, liberty, or anything else?

The attitude of the Loyalists to the King is expressed in a letter of Johanathan Sewell's, written from England in 1778,* in which he says he has both laughed and wept over his friend's letter, describing conditions in the Colonies. "Faith, I'll enclose it to Lord North to be communicated to His Majesty in

---
* Winslow papers.

private, and yet, God bless his good soul, why should I wish to make him cry? It is no fault of his this cursed rebellion was not suppressed long ago, unless you call mercy and tenderness in the extreme a fault."

The King also showed a royal sporting spirit when everything was over and the Treaty of Paris signed. When his gracious Majesty admitted John Adams to his Royal presence he said: "Sir, I was the last man in England to consent to the independence of the Colonies. Now that you have got it, sir, I shall be the last man to disturb it." There was no sound of tyranny in that Royal speech.

In contemplating this strange migration of the Loyalists, one thing is very apparent; it solved, in the best possible way, the problem of populating the newly-acquired British North America (then almost wholly French) with an infusion of loyal and most desirable British subjects.

How long before the close of the war far-seeing British leaders had realized this to be the cheapest and easiest way out of a rather hopeless entanglement, it is hard to say; letters at that period were very guarded. Men like Carleton, Cornwallis and Howe saw the hopeless task of subduing the rebel colonies, whose aim was independence, and who were only inflated to further wrath by offers of concessions. Even were they conquered they could not be subdued without a vast amount of troops and money that were sadly needed at home. It would be a wiser investment for England to leave these rebel colonies glorying in their victory, skim off the cream of the population that still remained loyal and remove it to the regions of Acadia, from which the French had lately been expelled. A better solution for their difficulties could never have been devised, and the rebels helped nobly about skimming the cream after the treaty of peace was signed. They organized companies and started societies for the purpose of harassing the Loyalists and driving them out of the country. For any kind of imaginary treason they were proscribed and banished; this, with the memory of ten years of nerve-wracking insecurity, made them thankfully accept offers of new lands in a new country, for they had learned to despise the land that had been their home. In letters of that period we find such sentences as these: "God grant that my next letter to you may be dated in some province rather to the northward of this." And another Loyalist writes, "As to Massachusetts Bay, I wish it well, but I wish never to see it again."

So came the Loyalists to those British provinces that had so lately been French—thirty thousand came to the old Acadia or Nova Scotia; others settled along the St. Lawrence and on the shores of the Great Lakes in what was then called Upper Canada.

All of which was known as His Majesty's possessions in North America. This now forms part of Canada.

4   THE PENOBSCOT LOYALISTS

NOW, the Loyalists who came to St. Andrews in that year of Grace, 1783, were not of the number that were organized under Sir Guy Carleton in New York. They were more a "private and personal" company that organized themselves under the name of "The Penobscot Loyalist Association", and thereby hangs a tale! All on account of an indefinite boundary line; but then, how in the world could boundaries be definite in those days of trackless forests? Well, it was like this: Nova Scotia was the old Acadia, at least it was supposed to extend indefinitely till it came to the equally indefinite boundaries of Massachusetts. Sunbury county answered for the vast tract north of the Bay of Fundy that now forms our neat little Province of New Brunswick.

The few scattered settlements along the coast of what is now the State of Maine vaguely considered the Penobscot the dividing line between Massachusetts and Nova Scotia. While the British flag waved over both indefinite boundaries, it did not matter much; in fact, it was often a convenience. Claims that were refused at Halifax could sometimes be dealt with at Boston and *vice versa*. Could any situation be more desirable?

However, when war clouds gathered and the sentiments of Whig and Tory, in the early '70s, became almost too well defined, boundaries began to mean something.

Nova Scotia was definitely British. The rebel leaders had, from time to time, made advances to her to join them, but were treated with silent disdain.

The Tories in the little town of Falmouth (now Portland), alarmed by the mutterings of their town-folk, decided, in the early days of unrest, to form a colony that would be more safely on British soil. Therefore, some of the prominent Tories of Falmouth started a settlement at Fort George, at the mouth of the Penobscot river, considering themselves thus within the Province of Nova Scotia.

Among them were three young men: Robert Pagan, an important merchant of Falmouth; Captain Wright, and Captain Wyer. The story of their undertaking is told in a letter (extracted from one of those hair trunks I before mentioned), written by Mr. Pagan to his wife, at Falmouth. There is, with this letter, another which I will also give on which Mr. Pagan has written: "Parting letter from my dear Mrs. Pagan —inclosing some of her lovely hair." The hair is still enclosed in the letter.

My dear Mr. Pagan

This day united us in the happy Bonds of wedlock. This Day seems Destained for us to Part for the first time, God forbid it should be a final separation. May we once more meet and be happy as we have ever ben.

May a gracious God Preserve and Protect my dearest Husband from the Dangers of the sea and from the sword of the enemy and from every evile.

It's hard to part, but it must be so. Go then my Dearest life and Prosper and may the God of all Grace be your

Confidence, may our constant Prayers to heaven be for each other's temporal and eternal happiness—fairwell

Yours Ever

M. PAGAN

The following letter, although only a fragment and unsigned, is written in Mr. Pagan's handwriting, and evidently sent to Mrs. Pagan, at Falmouth, in the December following the time of the above letter:

Fort George Penobscot 23rd December 17—

My dearest gerl—,

I wrote you of the 19th & 20th inst., informing you of our safe arrival here the 10th after an agreable passage.

I find this to be a most agreable situation even at this season, and I am confident that it must be much more so in summer. The house of Captn. Mowat's in which Captn. Wright, Captn. Wyer and I live, is glazed, clapboarded and shingled, but has no chimney nor a single room any way finished. Capn. Wright, before I came, had a room partitioned off for a store, and Hearth with a chimney built out of one of the windows which makes that place Tolerable warm. We have a place boarded off upstairs about the bigness of your room, in which we all sleep, and it is Close Borded as to be very comfortable.

I have got a very convenient store parted off in the opposite corner of the house from Capn. Wrights. Have laid a good floor for it and seiled it all over. I have also got it all shelved and a fine stove for it, so it is the best store and the most comfortable Room in the whole place. I have not yet been able to open any of my goods nor will I for some days as the getting the vessels dispatched requires my own and Capn. Wright's constant attention. Tho' there have several adventurers arrived with goods in two vessels lately from Halifax. Yet I find almost all the articles I brot. with me are in Demand. And as I have a much better assortment that was ever brot. here by one person, I have no doubt of getting a great part of the Custom, and selling to a good profit. I have also the

26

prospect of purchasing lumber, furs &ct to advantage, In short I hope and humbly trust that by the protection and Blessing of that kind and Merciful providence, who has from our Infancy made us both his peculiar care, I shall do well here and make a good winter's work of it.

It is probable that Capns. Wright, Wyer and I may be concerned in the purchase of one or two vessels, some lumber, furs &ct. during the winter, as it will not be in my power to make such purchases without their assistance, but what share I shall hold has not yet been talked of between us.

I think it is not probable that I shall come up in the spring unless there is a certainty of the Troops going to Falmouth. There is not at present a House in this whole town in which you could possibly live this winter as there is not one finished room in any of them. All the houses in the place are one story high except the one we live in, but if I resolve to stay here next summer (which if the Troops do not go to Falmouth I believe I shall) I will, in the spring, build a small house Which I can do at little expense, for your accommodation and that of your Father and Mother as I am convinced you will choose to come to this place in the spring and will be much pleased in its delightful situation.

Beef is very plenty here at 5d or 6d. currency per lb. also Mutton and at the same price. Butter 1/6 to 2/ per lb. Eggs 1/6 a doz. Wild Fowl 2/ per pair. Milk 6d per quart. Cranberries 10/ per bushel. potatoes & turnips 3/ per bushel. Cabbage, not large, 5/ per doz. all Halifax currency, we have also venison at 6d per lb.

By the schooner *Seafoam,* Capn. Bell, I intend to send you a kegg of pickled lobsters & some smoked salmon, some potatoes & turnips, some cranberries, some mackerel also a quarter of beef and a side of good mutton, while I shall procure in two or three days.

I have wrote Willie fully relating our little Garrison & several other matters, he will show you the letter.

I am not at all uneasy for our safety or that of our property. I Desire to commit myself, you my dearest, all ours and all that we possess to the protection of that God from whom we have recd. so many signal favors. who we can both, with pleasing satisfaction, say has hitherto helped us and who overrules the Turbulent dispositions of Men as he pleases. He has most mercifully brot. me here in a short and pleasant passage, given me pleasing prospects here and I trust will crown the undertaking with His goodness that our hearts may rejoice yet again in the possession of the blessing of his goodness.

Jonathan Tory, Mrs. Berry's brother, was at Falmouth about three weeks ago. He says all that family, Mrs. Berry, Mrs. Oxnard and all her friends, Mrs. Ross and her friends, Dr. Coffin and all our friends are well.

Mrs. Ross is not married, nor any foundation for the report.

I hope to be able to forward Mrs. Tyng's letter also Mr. Oxnard's in a few days and so inform our friends there of our arrival and all our welfare. I have met with several of the country people here with whom I used to trade. There is a son of Samuel Buckmans here called Sam. He tells me he has often made fun for you and Mrs. Wyer about some old man whose name I cannot recollect.

I have wrote night and day since I arrived here. Owing to a great deal of trouble we had had with the sailors. I shall be obliged to sett up pretty late, or rather early to get my letters done, to go by this opportunity. For this reason I have not wrote Mrs. Tyng nor Mr. Oxnard and did they know how much fatigue I have undergone and how late and early I have been at writing, ever since I arrived here I am sure they will freely excuse me. I will write them both fully by the schooner *Seafoam,* pleas tell them this and remember me affectionately to all friends. Captn. Wyer wrote Mrs. Wyer fully by this opportunity. I believe he means to settle here also in spring. I have endeavored to mention to you everything I can recollect and yet I am loathe to give over writing to you. The recollection of my pleasing . . . . .

The rest of this letter is missing. The "Willie" referred to is most probably a brother, William Pagan.

The Falmouth Loyalists had suffered much from enthusiastic rebels who, one wild night, led by a military gentlemen named Thompson, ran riot through the town with patriotic intentions of plundering the Tories, beginning with their wine cellars, after which they were in good shape for any form of destruction that came to hand, and by morning many important Falmouth Loyalists found themselves homeless.

Next day up came Captain Henry Mowat in a sloop of war, wanting to know what it was all about. This altered the aspect; the inhabitants, by the light of day, began to feel sober and nervous. They explained that some of their people, being rather under the influence of liquor, had got out of hand, as it were, and would the Captain be so kind and understanding as to show them leniency? So the Captain, who really had a kind heart, contented himself by taking on board all the homeless Loyalists he could find and sailing away, and the incident went down in history as "military occupation by Thompson".

That most uncomfortable incident, however, showed pretty well how the wind blew, and the little settlement on the other side of Penobscot grew apace. The inhabitants formed the Penobscot Loyalist Association, and many loyal refugees joined them there from all points, some coming even from Boston. There they lived in small, rapidly constructed, frame houses until the close of the war. In 1779 it was made a military post by the British, under command of General McLean.

That autumn up came Captain Mowat again to Falmouth, this time with orders to take the place. But no, Falmouth had no intention of giving up its guns; he had not been able to take them the last time and it was not likely he could do it again; in fact, they knew he was easy. But this time the Captain came with orders from headquarters and he had been easy long enough, so he opened fire and destroyed about one-fifth of the town, just to show it was time the other side was heard from. That was a different story altogether. It was all right for Tories to be robbed and homeless, but pious rebels should be spared these inconveniences— Cruel Tyrant! He actually *did* spare their church, but who asked him to do that? Who wants favours from tyrants? And, what is more annoying than coals of fire?

Well, there was nothing for it but to go and besiege the Tories at the Penobscot, and that was a real siege. Up came Captain Mowat again with the good ship *Albany* and others to help General McLean hold the fort, and they held it—held it till the very end of the war. Then, awful thought, what if the Penobscot should not be made the boundary? So the Penobscot Association (who were quite a strong force now, having been joined by so many other loyal souls) decided to send a representative to England to represent the situation at the fountain head.

Now, there was one John Calef, then acting as ship surgeon on board the *Albany*, considered to be a man of parts of pleasing address and persuasive manners, the very man to tell Lord North all the things he needed to know about boundaries.

So off went Dr. Calef across the sea to England, and Captain Henry promised to keep an eye on his wife and family who lived at Ipswich, in Massachusetts. Poor

Captain Henry, he had so many things to keep his eye on in those trying days of the War! However, he had a young cousin David who had a vessel of his own in the merchant service; he, therefore, asked him to keep his eye on Dr. Calef's family. So off sailed Captain David to Ipswich to see how Mrs. Calef and the children were getting on. But the pleasant land of Ipswich was not what it used to be; moreover, they knew all about the siege of Penobscot there and the havoc wrought at Falmouth, and anybody connected with that cruel old tyrant, Captain Henry, had better be taken prisoner. And so it fell out when the young captain did arrive at the happy little Calef home, in Ipswich, under cover of night, after many perilous adventures, he could not sit down by the fire and talk things over with the family, he had to be hidden away somewhere where no one would see him, sometimes in the attic, sometimes in the cellar, sometimes (when he needed air) in the woods beyond the house, or in the loft of the barn. Dr. Calef's little daughter Mehetible, only twelve years old, took his meals to these secluded spots.

When older people went out in those troubled times they might have stones thrown at them, and always there was the shout of "Tory! Tory!" waiting round the corner for everyone who loved his king and country; but a little girl, just twelve years old, was not so likely to be molested, and little Mehetible was not afraid. She was never afraid, all through her long eventful life she never knew fear. The young Captain could tell her lovely stories, too. Wild tales of the Orkney Islands, where he had spent his boyhood;

legends of courtly Spaniards wrecked on those rocky shores long ago from the Spanish Armada, who ever afterwards made their home among the Island people and from whom his family had descended. This tall swarthy weather-beaten sailor became a wonderful person in the eyes of the little Mehetible.

And all this time Dr. Calef was on his way to London to talk about boundaries with Lord North and other important people.

The war waged on. Danger for the Loyalists lurked at every turn. Mrs. Calef, fearing for the safety of her children, decided to take them to the peaceful and unquestionably British shores of the Bay of Fundy.

The young Captain would gladly take them in his boat. But no, the enemy was hot on his trail, and Mrs. Calef had another errand for him to do. He must take his boat and wait off the coast for the return of her husband and inform him of their whereabouts and bring him back to her at the Bay of Fundy.

So she hired a vessel and took her six children, the family Bible that had belonged to her father, (that good old minister of the gospel, Jedediah Jewett), and her armchair Grandmother Dummer gave her, and a silver tankard, and she packed them all on board with the furniture and other household goods and sailed away to that unknown shore.

Coming up the Bay of Fundy in a snow storm, the little craft bearing the Calef family lost its way and ran aground some miles from the mouth of the St. John River; she and the children had to walk through the storm, around the shore, till they found shelter in the small settlement that is now Saint John.

Meanwhile the end of the war had come with the Treaty of Paris, which severed the thirteen colonies, which were English, from British North America, which was entirely French. The cut was made with a dull knife and some of the edges were not well severed, and over in London Lord North was sadly explaining to Dr. Calef: "Doctor! Doctor! the pressure is too great, St. Croix must be the boundary not the Penobscot."

That was the word that came to the Penobscot Association in their newly established settlement. "Well", they said, "it is the ruling of a Divine Providence." And so they must move again. If the St. Croix was to be the boundary, to the St. Croix they would go, and they went.

Down came the little houses so hastily knocked together for their settlement at Fort George; all the frame-work, lumber and material, everything they had needed there, they would need likewise on the banks of the St. Croix. Furniture and silver and dishes and tools and livestock as well. Those little sailing ships must have been weighted to the water's edge with such varied and precious cargoes. Then the coffee-house had to come too, the coffee-house that had been the scene of many secret meetings of the Association, so many festive meetings too when it was used as the officers' mess. They could never get on without it. A bill for the removal of this little building is still in existence, which reads: "Estimates of the Coffee House,

with the expense of removing it to St. Andrews."
Andrew Martin to John McPhail

		£	s	d
Dr.				
To the House taken down at Penobscot		30	0	0
Freight from here to St. Andrews		13	10	0
Taking down 3,000 bricks		6	0	0
Freight *do* *do*		2	10	0
1,000 feet seasoned boards		2	10	0
Freight on *do*		1	10	0
4 window frames cases and sashes glazed		4	0	0
1 pannel door		1	0	0
		61	0	0

The Coffee House was then owned by John McPhail
and his wife, who ran it as a hospitable tavern. John
was away in England at the time and Mrs. McPhail
had much difficulty in superintending the removal,
and finally got involved in a law suit.

This interesting structure was unfortunately burned,
in 1930, when a disastrous fire broke out on Water
Street.

With everything on board, even to the Coffee
House, that courageous little fleet set sail to found
another settlement at the mouth of another river.
Anything for peace and the British flag. They had
previously sent out agents and a surveyor to inspect
the land about the mouth of the St. Croix, and had
heard pleasing reports of the present destination.

Of the advance guard was one James Maloney (then
spelled Malownay) who, with his family, settled on
the island now known as Navy Island, where he

was joined by others, and for many years there was a considerable settlement on this island. It is told of James Maloney that, on arriving, he let his little son cut down a small sapling so that he could say he cut the first tree in the new settlement. They feared to settle on the mainland, as the Indians were not particularly cordial. How eagerly must they have watched for the coming of the other vessels.

5   THE ARRIVAL

ON THE 3rd of October, 1783, the fleet from Penobscot rounded Clam Cove Head and sailed across the bay. Then, as though they had not enough discouragements, who should meet them but that notorious mischief maker, John Allen, with information that the destination they had chosen was American ground and they would have to go farther on to the Magaguadavic, which was the real St. Croix River. Fortunately, they paid little attention to this interruption. Possibly they were more familiar with the early French history of that region than John Allen; anyway, he had no papers to show, so on they sailed, on up to the harbour where the islands and wooded hill-sides all about welcomed them, that October day, with the royal colours of scarlet and gold. It must have seemed very peaceful after the stormy scenes they had left.

The ships anchored in the harbour, the small boats were lowered and the gallant gentlemen, in their powdered wigs and plum-coloured coats and three-cornered hats, helped the ladies to alight. How quaint and delightful a picture. Those courteous gentlemen and gentle and courageous ladies, in silks and quilted petticoats, tripping up over the sands to their new homes. Was there ever before so strange an exodus as that of the Loyalists? There they were with all their household goods, priceless mahogany and silver plate, damask and linen, family portraits, and heavy trunks, brass-studded and covered with calf skin, their servants and coloured slaves. All landed there on the red sandstone with the gorgeous forest back of them in the haze of a lovely Indian summer day, starting again to build them a city to dwell in. What a picture for Watteau or Fortuney.

It must have been fun, too. A kind of vast picnic for those courageous and resourceful people who, for the last ten years, had lived in constant dread of pillage and plunder, insult and abuse, with the derisive cry of "Tory" forever ringing in their ears. Here, in this place of peaceful Indian summer, all their friends with them, all their enemies left behind. Peace at last! That must have been a busy day, that first day. Shelter had to be provided for the night and for their property in case of rain, and fires had to be lighted too and food cooked, and trees had to be cut down, plenty of work for every one and no time to lament about hardships. All any one requires in this life is food and shelter, who would fuss about luxuries? The government supplied them with boards, nails and window glass, and rations of food were to be sent them through the winter. The forest supplied them with fuel. There were fish in the sea and wild fowl and deer in the woods, and they were safe on British soil, in spite of John Allen, and they had visions of founding a town after their own heart. Who would mind a few hardships? And that was the beginning of St. Andrews, Shiretown of Charlotte.

An old letter, written the following year by William Pagan to his friend Dr. Paine, who at that time was settled on an island near L'Etang (now known as Fryes Island), describes the efforts of those early days.

> William Pagan to Dr. William Paine*
> St. Andrews, 2nd May, 1784.
> Dear Sir,—
> I have just learned of your arrival at Harbor L'Etang and am in great hopes before you return to Halifax you will find time to pay our new settlement a visit. You will find us in a state of infancy, but when it is considered that there was not a single house erected till last October, you will not think lightly of our exertions.
> We have now about Ninety Houses up, and great preparations making in every quarter of the town for more. Numbers of inhabitants are daily arriving and a great many others are hourly looked for from different quarters. Agents are now here from the neighboring States on the look out for lands for a number of valuable inhabitants who wish to emigrate here, being tired of their new Government.
> I have not yet seen your part of the Bay, but from information the lands are good. I, early this spring, made one of an Exploring Party. We went all round Oak Point Bay, and up Scudock River as far as the Indian settlement a little above the Falls. These are part of the lands laid out for the Associated Loyalists from Penobscot and I can with pleasure assure you

---

* Winslow papers.

that the Land is in general very good, abounding with large Quantities of hard wood, all kinds of Pine Timber of a large growth and very handy to the water where most vessels can safely anchor. There are a number of Falls of water where Saw Mills can be erected, but only two on Scudock yet up. The Mill Priviliges on Oak Point Bay have been lately sold to defray the charges of the Town, the purchasers are making preparations to erect Saw Mills. The timber is very handy to the mills and no end to the quantity.

There is a large growth of White Pine fit for Masts & Spars of any dimensions. In fact from my own observation and from the information I have had from undoubted authority I am fully convinced that the Grand Bay of Passamaquoddy alone can supply the whole British West India Islands with Boards, Planks, Scantling, Ranging Timber, Shingles, Clapboards and every species of Lumber that can be shipped from New Brunswick, oak staves excepted. Masts, Spars and square timber, suitable for the British market, can be furnished to any extent from here, and nothing prevents these articles from being furnished in greatest abundance, of the best quality and on at least equal terms with any other part of the continent, but the want of Inhabitants and Saw Mills, in both which we have the most promising prospect of cutting a very respectable figure in the course of this year, 1784.

The easy navigation to this Town exceeds any I have seen; no person of any observation will want a pilot after being once up, and we are accessible at all seasons of the year.

The Fishery in this Bay you are no doubt sufficiently informed as to the great extent it can be carried on.

Excuse the liberty I have taken in giving my opinion of our new Settlement. I know you are interested in its prosperity and will be pleased with the accounts I have given, especially when I assure you that I am not governed by my own opinion alone, but also by the opinion of every person who has taken pains to explore this portion of the country.

Should your time not permit you to pay us a visit now, I am in hopes to have the pleasure of meeting you at St. Johns where I shall set out in a few days on my way to Halifax.

I am dear Sir
Your most obedient servant
WILL. PAGAN.

6 THE INDIANS

THE Loyalists were never troubled much by the Indians. They treated them kindly and met them on terms of equality and friendship and an Indian never forgets kindness neither does he presume on friendship.

There was a large encampment at that time and the natives looked on the arrival of so many white men with considerable apprehension at first. But it was not long before they were calling them brother and sister and if the Indians addressed any member of the colony (no matter how high in rank) by the Christian name, they were never corrected. This was a matter of expediency at first, later it became a matter of history, now it is a matter of family pride. But in those old days of such extreme formality when even near relatives and members of one family often avoided using the Christian name, this concession to the Indians seems quite remarkable.

A most picturesque pow-wow had taken place at Saint John some little time before the arrival of the Loyalists, and the Indians on that occasion promised their allegiance to King George, their "forgiving and affectionate father."

There had been considerable trouble with the Indians before this and, at the outbreak of the War, Washington had sent agents to enlist the services of the Indians of Nova Scotia and the River St. John, consequently the Indians took the summons as an excuse to rob and plunder wherever they felt disposed, and many isolated and defenceless settlements suffered in consequence.

Again we find that old trouble maker, John Allen, of Machias, with his finger in the pie. He wrote out a fine declaration of war for the Indians and sent them round to Saint John with it, bearing the British flag which had been given them and which he advised them to return. The declaration of war was a masterpiece in its way, it might be termed an Indian document with the colonial influence. So off went Pierre Thoma and his braves in ninety canoes, all painted up for war, and with the war cry of "Tory" that John Allen had taught them.

Michael Franklin, the commissioner of Indian Affairs, was there to meet them with two great friends of the Indians. One was Mr. James White, who for many years had engaged in friendly and profitable trading with the Indians, and the good and kindly Father Bourg, who had come to help them by request.

They talked things over pretty peacefully, then the Indians presented the declaration of war which read:

*"To the British Commanding Officer at the mouth of the St. John River:

"The Chiefs, Sachems and young men belonging to the River St. John have duly considered the nature of the Great War between America and Old England. They are unanimous that Old England is wrong and

---

* Raymond's History of the St. John River.

40

America is right. The River on which you are with your soldiers belongs from the most ancient times to our Ancestors, consequently is ours now, and which we are bound to keep for our posterity. You know we are Americans and this is our Native Country; You know the King of England, with his evil councillors, has been trying to take away the Lands and Liberty of our Country, but God, the King of Heaven, our King, fights for us and says America shall be free. It is so now in spite of all Old England and his comrades can do.

"The great men of Old England in this country told us that the Americans would not let us enjoy our religion; this is false, not true, for America allows everybody to pray to God as they please; you know Old England never would allow that, but says you must all pray like the King and the Great Men of his Court. We believe America now is right, we find all true they told us for our Father the King of France takes their part, he is their friend, he has taken the sword and will defend them. Americans is our friends, our Brothers and Countrymen.

"What they do we do, what they say we say, for we are all one and the same family.

"Now as the King of England has no business, nor never had any on this River, we desire you to go away with your men in peace and to take with you all those men that has been fighting and talking against America. If you don't go directly you must take care of yourself, your men and all your English subjects on this River, for if any and all of you are killed it is not

41

our faults, for we give you warning time enough to escape. Adieu for ever.

"Machias August 11th, 1778.

"Ankaque Pawhagen August 18th, 1778."

After a great deal of talk the Indians owned up that they had never found the English as bad as John Allen had painted them, and they owned to having been bribed to sign the declaration of war, and they also promised to restore some of the goods they had plundered.

After this happy agreement had been arrived at, Colonel Franklin thought it time to show John Allen what an Indian document looked like with a British influence, so he sat down and wrote a reply to the declaration.

"To John Allen and his associates at Machias. The Chiefs and Great men of the Malacete and Mickmack Indians hereby give thee notice. That their eyes are now open and they see already that thou has endeavored to blind them to serve thy wicked purpose against their lawful sovereign King George, our forgiving and affectionate Father.

"We have this day settled all misunderstandings that thou didst occasion between us and King George's men.

"We now desire that thee and Prebble and thy comrades will remain in your wigwams at Machias and not come to Passamaquoddy to beguile and disturb our weak and young Brethren. We will have nothing to do with thee or them or with your stories, for we have found you out, and if you persist in tempting us, we warn you to take care of yourselves. We shall not come to Machias to do you any harm, but beware of Passamaquadic, for we forbid you to come there.

"At Menaquashe the 24th September 1778.

"(Signed) Pierre Thoma, Francis Xavier

"Jean Batiste Arimph."

So the Indians took the oath and gave Colonel Franklin a string of wampum and also the presents Washington had sent them and the treaty they had made to furnish six hundred warriors for their war.

That wasn't all there was to it either, there had to be a war-dance and a vast number of ceremonies and the English did their part nobly and distributed presents in all directions, as the bills that still exist can show. Then who should come sailing up the harbour but Captain Henry in His Majesty's ship *Albany*. So they all had to go on board the *Albany* to drink the King's health, which any Indian is always ready to do for any King at any time, and Captain Henry gave them all a supply of gunpowder to subdue the King's enemies. Then there was more singing and dancing, and they all went off, escorted to the portage above the Falls by all the important people in the place, and the cannon on Fort Howe fired a salute and so did the good ship *Albany,* and the Chief and their braves gave a magnificent war whoop, and off they sailed up the river in their canoes. And from that time to this the Indians have been our friends, and it is not on record that John Allen ever returned to trouble the peaceful waters of Passamaquoddy. However, he still continued the writing habit, for it worried him very much to know that the loyal subjects of King George had taken possession of the St. Croix River when he was sure it was not the St. Croix River at all. So he wrote frantic letters to headquarters about it, but they were very busy at headquarters in those days and were quite used to frantic letters arriving from remote places, so no one paid much attention to the matter for some years to come.

Some of the Loyalists, however, did remove to the other side of the Magaguadavic and founded a settlement that they called St. George.

As to the Indians, they became more than friendly; they were sociable and liable to drop in any cold night and sleep in Loyalist kitchens before the great open fireplaces, wrapped up in their blankets. But they never stole anything or gave any trouble, and from them the new settlers learned many useful and interesting facts about their new home.

7 THE EARLY YEARS

IT REALLY was quite wonderful how quickly towns grew up; farms were cleared, ships were built and trade and commerce started in that land which, before the arrival of the Loyalists, had been an uninhabited wilderness.

The little town of St. Andrews grew rapidly. White-sailed ships darted in and out of the harbour, bearing cargoes of lumber and dried fish to the West Indies;

and returning with rum, molasses, fruits, indigo and spices. Cargoes of furs and lumber went to England, the vessels bringing back merchandise of all kinds.

Mr. Pagan and his brother William set up their store close to the water's edge and started trading on an extensive scale.

Charles Morris, a son of the Surveyor-General, laid out the town for them in neat square town lots stretching for a mile along the water front and up the sloping hillside. Every one received a grant of a town lot and a strip of wild land further out in the country, or else an island or a part of an island. It was a most exciting time, every day ships arrived with news and stores and people. The government made generous provisions for them during these early days and everybody worked hard. The gentlemen were forced to lay aside their plum-coloured coats and silk stockings, and wore worsted and deer skin when they went on exploring parties through the densely wooded country. Ladies were obliged to use mahogany tables in their kitchens, also their best silver and china. They had been unable to bring much besides their most treasured possessions. To this day some old tables bear the marks of pots and flat irons, and crested silver spoons are worn from scraping porridge pots in the early days.

Altogether they were a very happy little community. Plenty of work and no luxuries, pleasant friends and a lovely land to live in, the British flag above them and King George on his throne across the sea, grateful for their loyalty and ready to help them. Was there ever such an ideal combination of circumstances to afford happiness to any little town? And the King issued a proclamation that they were to be called the "United Empire Loyalists," and that they could sign the letters U.E.L. after their worthy names, they and their descendants, for ever and ever.

One day during the first winter of their exile, two Indians came tramping into town—an Indian and a squaw. They had come through the Maine woods and crossed the river farther up on the ice, so they said, but when they got to Mr. Pagan's store a cry of joy went up—they were not Indians at all, but Dr. John Calef back again, safe and well, and the swarthy young Captain with him, who really did look very like an Indian. They had been forced to land further down the coast and had walked through on snow shoes, protected by their disguise.

Where did they find Mrs. Calef and the children? Were they still in Saint John? History is a little vague, but the chances are that Mrs. Calef had by that time joined the Doctor's friends at St. Andrews to wait her husband's return. He had been gone four years, during which time communication by letter had been almost impossible. Letters in those days went not by mail, but by "opportunity." It must have been a happy day for the good Doctor and his family, and little Mehetible (now sixteen years old) found the Captain more enchanting than ever.

For the first year after the coming of the Loyalists St. Andrews was in the County of Sunbury and the Province of Nova Scotia, and all legal and government business was transacted with Governor Parr at Halifax. This was inconvenient, for Halifax was a long way off, but the following year a plan was brought forward to form a separate province on this side of the Bay of Fundy. After some opposition, this was put through and they called the new province New Brunswick, after the House of Brunswick, in honour of the King, and they divided it up into a convenient number of counties, and the one St. Andrews was in was called Charlotte, after the Queen.

The inhabitants of St. Andrews were consulted before the change was made, and the following letter expresses their sentiments:

*Representation of the inhabitants of St. Andrews
St. Andrews, 26th May 1784.

Gentlemen,—We had the honour to receive your favour of the 18th current with the enclosures and have laid them before the Inhabitants of this town at a Meeting called for the purpose of considering the same.

We have the Pleasure to acquaint you that the Meeting were unanimous in the opinion of the inconveniency and disadvantages arising to the Inhabitants on the North side of the Bay of Funday by the distance from Halifax, the present site of Government, and sensible of the great advantages which would attend the Establishment of a New Province to comprehend all the settlements on the North Side of the Bay, and they earnestly wish that the application for that purpose, which appears to be the general voice of the Inhabitants may be attended to by the British Legislature.

Altho the first settlers only arrived here in October last (1783), yet we have already sent a number of Cargoes of lumber to the West Indies and several ports in Nova Scotia, and as more Saw Mills are now erecting, our Exports of Lumber will rapidly increase.

All our Inhabitants earnestly wish that the British Legislature may in their wisdom think proper to continue to these

---

* Winslow papers.

Provinces the exclusive privileges of supplying the British West Indies with Fish and Lumber, and also grant to them Bountys on the Exportation of these articles, which will greatly add to the encouragement of our Trade and Fishery.

We have wrote you thus fully at the unanimous desire of the Inhabitants of St. Andrews at their Meeting this day.

And have the Honour to be, Gentlemen

Your most obedient and Hum. Servants

      ROBERT PAGAN
      COLIN CAMPBELL
      WILLIAM GALLOP
      JER. POTE

To Messrs Frederick Hauser, George Leonard, William Tyng, Thos. Horsefield, Bartholomew Crannel, James Peters & William Hazen; Agents for the Loyalists on the St. John River.

The date at the head of the above letter is May 26th, 1784, the very day on which Captain Nehemiah Marks and members of his party left St. Andrews and sailed up the Schoodic to found the town of St. Stephen.

The four gentlemen who signed this letter were all prominent in public affairs in St. Andrews in the early days.

Mr. Robert Pagan carried on business in St. Andrews, while his brother William finally settled in Saint John. Robert was a shrewd and clever merchant and gave the Lord all the credit for his success.

The Brig *Miriam* (called after his dear wife) flitted back and forth from Grenada and other ports of the West Indies. He purchased forest lands in all the accessible portions of the province, and left a considerable estate when he died. Those primeval forests could so readily be turned into gold in the old days of shipping, when men built and owned their own vessels and no one fussed about freight rates.

The Robert Pagans had no children, but two little girls, the daughters of Thomas Pagan, lived with them; they also brought up a daughter of Colonel Wyer's after his wife died. These three girls—Margaret, Maria and Miriam, lived with them until they married, receiving all the care and kindness this generous, kindly couple could bestow upon them.

Mrs. Pagan's old father and mother, Mr. and Mrs. Jeremiah Pote, lived near them in one of those same little cottages that had been brought from Penobscot. Mr. Pote must have been a delightful old gentleman and the honoured patriarch of the town. He owned a piece of ground on the upper part of King Street, which he presented to the town for a burying ground. And there it stands to this day.

Sadly enough, almost the first person to be laid there was his youngest son, Robert, then a promising youth of 25 years of age; that was in November, 1794.

A quaint letter from Mrs. Pagan still exists, written at this time to her nephew Jeremiah Pote Wyer, who was then on a voyage in the Brig *Miriam* with Captain McArthur. The letter is addressed:

Mr. Jere. J. Wyer
  Mate of the Brig "Miriam". London
  St. Andrews December 21st, 1794

ir Jerry,
  Your Uncle J.J.P. hath wrote you some time ago by
  tain Watt that was bound to the North Side of Jamaica,
  e I trust you are arrived long ere this.

Little did I then think I should have so soon to write you on a subject so Distressing and Melloncholy as the death of your Dear Uncle Bobby. He sailed from this on the 6th of August to Bermudas, but missing the Island after some time, went on to Kingston in Jamaica, where he sold his cargo. He was in perfect health while there and sailed for home on the 29th of October, the very day you left this—on the 5th of November was taken ill with the fever and died on the 8th— he had his senses part of the time of his illness, and expected not to live. One of the Hands (a stranger) died two days after him. On the 7th of December the Brig arrived here with the dismal and heavy tidings.

Your poor grandfather and grandmother are in great affliction and I fear it will bring down their grey hairs with sorrow to the grave. I do all I can to comfort them and endeavor to keep up their spirits, but I fear they will sink under the weight of sorrow. They have lost a dear and only son, the support and comfort of their declining years, on whom the hopes of their old age was fixed, one in the bloom of life and vigor of Health and bid fair to see many days.

O, my Dear Jerry, may this striking instance of mortality teach you to remember your Creator in the days of your youth, to put your trust in God as your only hope thro' time and eternity— be not influenced by any example to sin against Him, allways remember that his eyes are upon you thro' life who will be your judge at death—to that God who is able to keep you I desire to commit you and pray he will Preserve you from sin and every danger and return you in safety to your parents.

Your father has wrote you by this opportunity as will your uncle. I hope this will find you well and safe arrived in London. Tell Capt. Bell his family is well. Remember me to Billy, tell him I hope he will be a good boy, it depends on his own conduct whether he will be a Credit or a Disgrace to his connections.

We are all in Health. You will no doubt meet the "Hope" in London if you both arrive safe, as she sailed from Jamaica in the same fleet as the "Harmony" for home. I have nothing

50

more to add but my best wishes for your Health and Safety and am,

Dear Jerry, your
Affectionate Aunt
M. PAGAN

Your grandfather and grandmother send their kind love to you.

We could wish that dear Mrs. Pagan had in this letter told Jerry something more of the life of the town as well as matters concerning his spiritual welfare. But he may have needed these admonitions for he too came to an early grave.

Poor old Mr. Pote did not long survive his son; he died two years later and was himself laid to rest in the plot of land he had given for a burying place.

Colin Campbell was another merchant who had business interests both in St. Andrews and Saint John. At that time it was not clear which would become the more important place. For some time they were keen rivals. Saint John won in the end, however, probably owing to the greater importance of its river.

Colonel Wyer was another important figure in those early days. He is the same Wyer who was associated with Robert Pagan in the Penobscot colony; his first wife was a daughter of Jeremiah Pote. He was the first Sheriff of the town and also Justice of the Peace. In the days before the war he had been customs officer at Falmouth.

Two brothers, Daniel and James McMaster, had come from Boston to join the Penobscot Loyalists; they also carried on business in various parts of the country, trading and lumbering.

Then there was Mr. Robert Garnett, who lived at the head of the town by the water front in a little house which no longer stands there, the material for which had been brought from Penobscot by a man named Maxwell, from whom Mr. Garnett purchased the building. He was the first judge of probate and acted as deputy under Edward Winslow.

Mr. Thomas Tomkins built his house at the top of King Street near where the large Elm stands. His daughter married Thomas Wyer, a son of the Colonel.

Mr. John Dunn, another prominent figure in those days, was the first Comptroller of the customs. He had come with the New York Loyalists and brought the material for a two storey house, the first to be erected in St. Andrews. He must have been a benevolent gentleman, for in his will he left a fund to be distributed to the poor of the town at Christmas—the fund is still used for that purpose.

A letter among some of his old papers gives an idea of the way they did business in those days. It is from his agent in the West Indies and bears the rather indefinite address.

Mr. JOHN DUNN,
Merchant
New York or Nova Scotia.

The letter is dated Kingston, Jamaica, 14th June, 1784:

Mr. John Dunn—
Sir,—
Having forwarded duplicate and triplicate of my respects to you of the 3rd inst., which related entirely to Insurance

52

on the "Lord Howe"; I do not now trouble you of another copy of it as this goes by Capt. McLean in that Vessell which I hope will arrive safe with you to a good market.

Enclosed you will please receive Invoice and bill of lading for 4 Hogsheds fine sugar, 16 punchs and Hhds of rum shiped on board her.

On your account and risque amounting to £425/0/10 Jamaica Currency at your debit in Acct Current which is also enclosed; and credited with £389/13/10½ Nett proceeds of her cargo from Penobscot and £806/13 Jamaica Currency for her Chartered Voyage to Georgia and back.

You will find £260 at the debit of this acct. for the cost of 5 New Negroes ship'd to Georgia for your account, which with my advances for the Vessel, leaves a ballance of £286/7/0½ in your favour; which last mentioned sum I have paid Capt. McLean to enable him to settle with the People and for other disbursements.

As the Vessell has really made money by her Voyage here, I have no doubt of your hearty approbation;—and as Capt. McLean has spared no pains for your interests, I flatter myself you will also approve of his services.

In the Expectation of hearing from you upon the arrival of the "Lord Howe"

I remain with Respect, Sir
Your Most Obed't Servant
JOHN MOORE.

We may be quite certain that the *Lord Howe* arrived safely in St. Andrews with the sixteen puncheons of rum, rather than in New York, and it was probably a merry day for the Loyalists. She had gone down to Jamaica the previous February loaded with "74 bundles of fish, 26 thousand of lumber, 2200 red oak staves, 135 old punchion packs and a parcell of hand-spikes and poles." Those were great days! And what a thrilling moment when one's ship came in!

Mr. Dunn also held the important office of High Sheriff of Charlotte and was later succeeded by Mr.

Elisha Andrews, a son of good old Parson Andrews.

The Deputy Sheriff at this time was one David Craig; he had come with the Penobscot Loyalists, and one of his arduous duties was to convey prisoners and mail between St. Andrews and Fredericton.

His descendants still recount traditional tales of these thrilling expeditions; of how David Craig with his prisoners would camp on winter nights beside a fire that had to be constantly kept burning to scare away the hungry wolves, and when the fire got low he would wave a burning brand that showed rows of little bead-like wolf eyes glaring at them from the forest. There was no fear of prisoners escaping on such expeditions. David Craig afterwards bought land at Chamcook, and there his descendants still live.

There was a considerable settlement on Navy Island at that time. The Maloney family, who first settled there, were joined by the Stinson family and others; descendants of both these families are living in St. Andrews to-day, and the sand bar at the entrance to the harbour owes its name to the Loyalist William Stinson and is still known as Billy's bar.

In those days the harbour light was a candle set in a lantern and hung on a post.

Dr. John Calef, after his return, also took an important part in the life of the town. His prolonged stay in England (a great experience in those days) had given him an insight into many things and he was much looked up to in the little colony.

He had much to tell them of his visit to London. Most important information of all was the intimation that England would try and repay those Loyalists who had suffered most heavily from loss of property during the Revolution—most joyful news! "It is the King's doings," they said. "Long live King George! Bless his kind soul."

Dr. Calef had another pretty story to tell. Once when attending a court function he had been introduced to the "pious and amiable" Selina, Countess of Huntington, and had told her about the little settlement at Penobscot and the losses and persecution of the King's loyal subjects in North America. So she promised to send out some Bibles and hymn books to his people, if he would let her know where they had finally settled. And this she did as soon as she heard from the Doctor about the founding of St. Andrews. A letter from this gracious lady was long in the possession of descendants of the Calef family.

Dr. Calef lived in Saint John for a time after his return, where he was appointed Surgeon to the garrison at Fort Howe. And in Saint John, in the year 1786, little Mehetible Calef married the Captain. She was just eighteen and he was twenty years older. The Rev. Mr. Bissett married them, and the bridesmaid was Anne Hecht, whose father was also connected with the garrison at that time.

The little bridesmaid has left us an interesting manuscript connected with this wedding, a poem written on birch bark giving the youthful bride some excellent advice and showing a rather interesting picture of the part a wife was expected to play in those early days.

POEM WRITTEN TO MEHETIBLE CALEF, ON HER MARRIAGE
TO CAPTAIN DAVID MOWAT, COMPOSED BY HER BRIDESMAID,
ANNE HECHT, IN THE YEAR 1786.

Advice to Mrs. Mowat

Dear Hetty—

Since the single state
You've left to choose yourself a mate,
Since metamorphosed to a wife,
And bliss or woe insured for life,
A friendly muse the way should show
To gain the bliss and miss the woe.
But first of all I must suppose
You've with mature reflection chose.
And thus premised I think you may
Here find to married bliss the way.
Small is the province of a wife
And narrow is her sphere in life,
Within that sphere to walk aright
Should be her principal delight.
To grace the home with prudent care
And properly to spend and spare,
To make her husband bless the day
He gave his liberty away,
To train the tender infant's mind,
These are the tasks to wives assigned.
Then never think domestic care
Beneath the notice of the fair.
But matters every day inspect
That naught be wasted by neglect.
Be frugal (plenty round you seen)
And always keep the golden mean.
Let decent neatness round you shine
Be always clean but seldom fine.
If once fair decency be fled
Love soon deserts the genial bed.
Not nice your house, though neat and clean
In all things there's a proper mean.
Some of our sex mistake in this;
Too anxious some—some too remiss.
The early days of married life

56

Are oft o'er cast with childish strife
Then let it be your chiefest care
To keep that hour bright and fair;
Then is the time, by gentlest art
To fix his empire in your heart.
For should it by neglect expire
No art again can light the fire.
To charm his reason dress your mind
Till love shall be with friendship joined.
Raised on that basis t'will endure
From time and death itself secure.
Be sure you ne'er for power contend
Or try with tears to gain your end
Sometimes the tears that dim your eyes
From pride and obstancy arise.
Heaven gave to man unquestioned sway.
Then Heaven and man at once obey.
Let sullen looks your brow ne'er cloud
Be always cheerful, never loud.
Let trifles never discompose
Your temper, features or repose.
Abroad for happiness ne'er roam
True happiness resides at home.
Still make your partner easy there
Man finds abroad sufficient care.
If every thing at home be right
He'll always enter with delight.
Your presence he'll prefer to all,
That cheats the world does pleasure call.
With cheerful chat his cares beguile
And always greet him with a smile,
Never with woe his thoughts engage
Nor ever meet his rage with rage.
With all our sex's softening art
Recall lost reason to his heart.
Thus calm the tempest in his breast
And sweetly soothe his soul to rest.
Be sure you ne'er arraign his sense,
Few husbands pardon that offence,
T'will discord raise, disgust it breeds
And hatred certainly succeeds.

Then shun, O shun that hated self,
Still think him wiser than yourself.
And if you otherwise believe
Ne'er let him such a thought perceive.
When cares invade your partner's heart
Bear you a sympathetic part.
. . . . (*illegible*) . .
From morn till noon, from noon till night
To see him pleased your chief delight.
And now, methinks, I hear you cry;
Shall she presume—Oh vanity!
To lay down rules for wedded life
Who never was herself a wife?
I've done nor longer will presume
To trespass on time that's not your own.

                                    ANNE HECHT

There is a letter accompanying this poem, but only
a part of it is legible, the birch bark having crumbled
away from weight of years. It begins:

> You will perceive, my dear Hetty, from the note of these
> lines, that you ought to have had them on that most important
> day of your life. But a thought popped into my head that your
> mind would be too much engaged (Twas very probable) and
> my sage notions would be thrown by even without one attentive
> reading. I had a mind, therefore, to wait till the hurry of the
> wedding was over and you became somewhat more domestic.
> You know what has happened since! and though perhaps a
> matron will think the preparation for a ball of no consequence,
> that must be my excuse for not offering these lines to you
> before . . . . .

*The rest of the letter is missing, but the closing words are
clear:*

> Wishing as long as you live that you may have happiness
>   One of the sincerest of your friends
>   ANNE HECHT

The little bride lived on in Saint John for some years.
Her first children were born there and two little boys,

58

Spencer and Ryder, died there. A memory of this period of her life has come down to us in a scrap of folded paper on which is written "my dear Spencer's ring and hair." A few years later she joined her father's family in St. Andrews, where she lived for the remainder of her long eventful life and brought up a large family.

Dr. Calef's son, Jedediah Jewett Calef, settled on one of the islands now known as Fryes Island. There he lived the life of a hermit, coming occasionally to St. Andrews to visit the family and borrow reading matter. He seems to have spent his life reading and developing the fishing industry among the islands. The Iliad and Odyssey, as translated by Pope, were his favourites in literature. He would tell the stories over and over to his many nieces and nephews when he visited St. Andrews, and they got the adventures of Ulysses all mixed in their minds with the adventures of the Loyalists.

Now it happened that, after the dust of war had settled and George Washington was firmly seated in the Presidential chair, he repented of the persecution of the Loyalists and awoke to the fact that, with the use of a little tact, they might have been turned into desirable citizens for his new Republic. Accordingly, he proclaimed that all those who wished to return would be given protection and their property returned to them. Few, however, availed themselves of this invitation. They were now enjoying some degree of comfort in their new homes. Besides, it was too soon. The old wounds were not yet healed. But Jedediah Jewett had pleasant recollections of goodly lands held by his father in the State of Massachusetts, in the vicinity of Rowley and Ipswich. He resolved to accept the invitation. His declining years required more comforts than his island home afforded and forthwith he went. But he soon returned—they had called him "Old Tory Calef." He preferred to come back to the screaming seagulls that circled round his little island kingdom.

When Dr. Calef came to St. Andrews, he built a house at the head of Water Street and planted a row of elms along the water front. He had begged for a release from his duties at the garrison, as he wished to remain with his family in St. Andrews, his wife being in failing health and there was no resident doctor. The doctor carried on some interesting experiments in inoculation for small-pox, as the following letter shows, written to Colonel Hailes at the Garrison:

* Sir,—Sometime back I did myself the honour to write a letter to you and enclosed a bottle containing a thread of pock matter which if not made use of I can get some fresh matter in this City and will send it if wanted, and should have much pleasure in assisting any of your family and friends through the small-pox.

I have the satisfaction to mention, Sir, that upwards of 500 persons in the town of St. Andrews and its neighborhood have had the small-pox since May last, in the natural way and by inoculation and but three only may be said to have died with the small-pox, and those were refractory children that would take no food other than what they chose, and no medicine whatever; four others have died but their deaths were after they had gotten over the small-pox.

---

* Winslow papers.

60

In this business I have been assisted by Madam Pagan, Col. Wyer, Henry Brown Esq. who performed the operation both in their own families and that of some of their friends but were thrown back in several cases where the disorders ran high, which gave much trouble to a physician by their setting out ignorantly in treating the disease; several of their adult patients were incrusted as with a coat of mail and when the crust fell off their appearance was like unto fleased rabbits but recovered.

Another picturesque figure also arrived in St. Andrews about this time, in the person of Colonel Christopher Hatch. He had come from Boston with the Loyalists to Saint John and was granted land there, but later obtaining a military appointment in St. Andrews, he moved there with his family, built himself a large brick house, where he lived in much elegance and dispensed a royal hospitality. He was also made a magistrate and had been commended for gallantry in the late war, where he had been wounded. Among his various retainers was an old coloured slave named Violet, who was unsurpassed as a cook and served up many a sumptuous dinner for the Colonel's parties. This old woman lived to a great age and was in later days a source of much interesting information of Revolutionary times.

8 THE BOUNDARY LINE

THE little town was now assuming some importance in the New Province. The men who had landed on those uninhabited wooded shores were now appointed to offices of trust. Mr. Gallop was recorder of wills and deeds. Colonel Wyer was Sheriff, Mr. Dunn Comptroller of Customs, and Mr. Pagan represented the County of Charlotte in the House of Assembly.

The New Province was a great success. Sir Guy Carleton had produced a brother (Sir Thomas), who was appointed Governor. And a site was chosen in the centre of the province, on the River St. John, for the seat of government and given the name Fredericton. It was rather inaccessible in those days when there were no roads and the river frozen over. There is a legend that Mr. Pagan, the member for Charlotte, tramped to Fredericton through the woods with an Indian guide, and it is on record that he was always in his place when the House met.

The only disturbing element in the peace of the community was an occasional letter from Governor Hancock, requesting that the entire population be removed to the other side of the Magaguadavic River, as they were occupying American territory. But the inhabitants of St. Andrews thought they knew their French history better than Mr. Hancock, so they stayed where they were. Finally, Governor Carleton arranged that a Commission be appointed to look into the question of the boundary. It was agreed that three Commissioners be appointed. Thomas Barclay was to represent the British and David Howell the United States and Egbert Benson, of New York, was chosen as a third member for the Commission. Robert Pagan and Joseph Garnet, of St. Andrews, were chosen as sub-agents to take evidence, and Phineas Bruce and John Cooper, of Eastport, sub-agents for the United States.

An old manuscript among the Winslow papers gives the following items:

This province has become of so much consequence to Great Britain and increasing daily in its magnitude that no time ought to be lost in establishing the boundary laid between the United States of America. The Americans claim the town of St. Andrews built since the Peace by the Loyalists, consisting of six hundred houses, together with many valuable islands in the Bay of Passamaquoddy, which by the express word of the treaty are clearly within the limits of New Brunswick. The inhabitants of St. Andrews and its vicinity amount to upwards of three thousand. If these Loyalists should fall with their properties within the limits of the States of America it is necessary that they should know it before any further improvements are made by them, as I believe not one of the families would remain subject to the States being perfectly happy under the government of Great Britain. It is the more necessary that this enquiry be immediately made while the Indians are alive that have been called up to Boston to give their evidence which is to remain on the records there, which river was anciently called St. Croix. They have declared upon their return that they were bribed to say the easternmost river. And it is the more necessary while the Old English and French inhabitants who have resided there upwards of forty years, can personally attend and give their evidence to the contrary. I have later been there and have examined the rivers, Islands, etc. and conversed with the old inhabitants and Indians; there can remain no doubt but the boundary line we claim is just and agreeable to the Treaty.

Well, the Commission first met at Halifax (one rather wonders why); next it met at St. Andrews, and Ward Chipman and Edward Winslow came down from Saint John and they held the meeting at Mr. Pagan's house, and there came the old traders who had come before the Loyalists, and the old Indians, and the Frenchman La Coote to interpret for them. An interesting assembly it must have been, all sitting there on the best chairs in Mrs. Pagan's best parlour.

La Coote himself was a romantic personality, being a French nobleman who had married an Indian girl and adopted the life and customs of her tribe. Four hundred guests had assembled for their wedding, and the festivities lasted night and day for four weeks. All of this lavish entertainment La Coote paid for handsomely. He certainly was entitled to a seat at the commission on one of Mrs. Pagan's best chairs.

It appeared from the evidence that the Magagua-davic had evidently been mistaken for the St. Croix by some of the early settlers who had fallen into the habit of calling it the St. Croix. John Allen had been very particular about this, and had evidently done much to help the memories of the Indians in this respect. Champlain's records had stated that quantities of fish were to be found during the spring below the Falls of the St. Croix. When Mr. Pagan questioned the Indians about the fish, they were quite willing to give the Schoodic (or St. Croix) River rather than the Magaguadavic, as the place where fish abounded in spring. John Allen, not knowing this fine point, had neglected to warn his pupils. When the evidence was taken, the meeting adjourned and it was decided to send to France for Champlain's map of St. Croix Island and compare it with the island at the mouth of the Schoodic River. This was done.

One day Mr. Pagan made a pilgrimage to the island, armed with Champlain's map, and accompanied by William Cookson, Thomas Greenlaw, Nehemiah Gilman and John Rigby. He evidently crossed over in a boat from the Bayside. They found the outline of the island, its rocks and shoals, agreed in every respect with Champlain's map. They landed on the island and found the ruins of the Fort just where Champlain had marked them. They found other relics too, part of a stone pitcher, bricks and charcoal.

On another occasion Mr. Pagan visited the island "on a pleasure trip," and again went to view the ruins; this time he had with him John Brown, the Rev. Mr. Andrews, Daniel McMaster, John Campbell, Donald McLaughlin, Donald Grant, William Pagan and Thomas Pagan. This time they did considerable digging and turned up a metal spoon, a musket ball, a piece of an earthen dish and an iron spike, "all bearing marks of having laid a long time in the ground."

All this was evidence enough for any Commission, but they had to have some more meetings about it, and finally they all went to Providence, in 1796, to see what John Adams had to say about it. And about the year 1798, the St. Croix was definitely accepted as the boundary line between the two countries, and that was as far as it went, which was not very far, for there were the Quoddy Islands at one end of the disputed line and the forests of Aroostook at the other, all waiting to make trouble at a later date. Which all goes to show that people who make treaties should be very particular about boundaries.

9 THE CHURCHES

THE Loyalists, being above all things a God-fearing race, soon began to think of establishing a church at St. Andrews. A very fine young clergyman, the Rev. Samuel Andrews, had joined their number in the year 1786, having come from Connecticut with two other clergy of the Church of England, Mr. Richard Clark and Mr. James Scovil.

Mr. Clark was sent to the Parish of Gagetown and afterwards removed from there to St. Stephen. Mr. Scovil went to the Parish of Kingston, where he was succeeded by his son and grandson.

Mr. Andrews purchased the island, still known as Minister's Island, from the original grantee named Osborn and then returned to Connecticut to get his family and belongings; he also brought with him the beautiful carved Royal Coat of Arms from the Town of Wallingford, his former parish in Connecticut. The parishioners had saved it from rebel hands, so eager to destroy anything of British origin, and they presented it as a parting gift to their good rector. And it remains to this day over the west door of All Saints Church.

They built a church for Parson Andrews to preach in, and a quaint little building it was too, with its squat bell tower and high pews. It stood by the alley-way still known as Church Lane, near the present site of the Andraeleo Hall. The present All Saints Church was not built till 1867.

In this little church Parson Andrews held service on Sundays, riding over from the island, his good wife, Hannah Anne, behind him on a pillion, across the bar and around by the shore (for there was no Bar Road in those days) every Sunday for thirty-two years. No wonder his tombstone records "a well spent life and a faithful ministry."

The first Church-wardens of the Parish were: Thomas Wyer and Joseph Garnet. The vestrymen were: John Hall, Maurice Salt, John Dunn, James Pendlebury, John Bentlay, William Gallop, and Joseph Garnet, vestry clerk.

After the death of Parson Andrews, in the year 1818, at the ripe age of 82, the Rev. Dr. Jerome Alley became Rector. He was a small plump gentleman who spoke with a lisp and inclined to be somewhat pompous. For forty long years he led the people of St. Andrews in the paths of righteousness. He was not beloved by his congregation as Parson Andrews had been, but they respected the dignity of his office and that answered the purpose in those days. His favourite doctrine was "Do ath' I 'thay not ath' I do."

This story is told of old Parson Alley and it is probably true. It seems he was in the habit of periodically holding service at Campobello. One Sunday morning he sent a little black boy down to the wharf with a peremptory demand to one Captain Paul to delay sailing for the island till he should be ready to go down with him.

The little darky returned from his errand and slipped into church while the old doctor was in the midst of his sermon. He had taken for his subject St.

Paul's famous reply to Agrippa, which he was vehemently expounding: "And what did Paul say?" he asked his hearers feelingly, repeating the question several times, just to make it impressive. When finally he thumped the pulpit and demanded loudly, "What did Paul say?" the little black boy got up and told him, so that every one could hear. "Paul said you never paid him for the last time and he'd be blowed if he'd take yer again!" It was a very trying moment for a decorous congregation.

The next sacred building to be erected in St. Andrews was the Kirk. There were a number of Scotch families in the place and much Scottish sentiment. They had all sat contentedly under good old Parson Andrews, but they now craved a church of their own. With Scotch thrift they saved their pennies till they grew to pounds, they bought the land and started the building, but by the time it was boarded in, the funds gave out and there it stood just like that for several years. Sometimes when it was not too cold they held services there, but it was rather forlorn; sometimes they used the Ordway Hall (now owned by the Knights of Pythias)—that was rather forlorn, too; sometimes they gave up and went to hear Parson Alley, and that did not prove very inspiring either.

In the end, however, one of Parson Alley's flock unwittingly lifted them out of their difficulties and at a dinner party made some insinuating remark about the unfinished condition of the new Kirk. This roused the indignation of a wealthy old Scottish merchant, Christopher Scott, and he handsomely offered to finish the building of the Kirk at his own expense.

Not only would he finish it, but he would make it the handsomest church in all His Majesty's dominions in North America. He sent to Scotland for designs and to the West Indies for mahogany and the forests of Charlotte yielded their best bird's-eye maple for the great pillars supporting the galleries. He assembled the most skilful workmen and the choicest materials. Everything must be perfect after its kind. A Moses building a tabernacle in the wilderness, while men looked on and wondered. In the corner of the ceiling huge plaster thistles grew, Scots thistles—one in each corner. The pulpit was a masterpiece of mahogany and bird's-eye maple most cunningly set together without nails or hammer. The work was done by Gordon Gilchrist, a clever carpenter.

Outside, the graceful steeple rose far into the sky with its gilded vane showing how the wind blew. On the front of the tower was painted a spreading oak tree, emblem of Greenock, Scotland, the home of Christopher Scott. Around the tree was written the name "Greenock Church" and the date: "finished June, 1824," and there it is to this day, high above the lovely door-way that would do credit to a Grecian temple. About the churchyard, oak trees were planted; then the work of Christopher Scott was complete. It was indeed a beautiful building. The delighted Presbyterians sent over to Glasgow University for a minister, the very best that could be had, to be sent out on the very first ship that sailed. And out came the Rev. Alexander McLean, with a splendid big pulpit Bible under his arm that was presented, as the inscription still shows, by "The Rev.

Dr. Davidson, of Edinburg, to the Scotch Church of St. Andrews, New Brunswick, May, 1824."

This Bible was placed on the uppermost deck of the enormous pulpit and there, for over a hundred years, Scottish divines in black robe and Geneva bands, against a background of crimson curtains, have read from that same ancient Bible, resting on its crimson velvet cushion, and prayed that the Lord would add a blessing to the reading of His word. The same benevolent gentleman in Edinburgh also presented the church with a solid silver communion service.

It would seem that nothing more could be desired. But, as in the wilderness of old, the people murmured against their Moses. There was some justification for their murmuring, and they did it with extreme politeness. They made so bold as to write Christopher Scott, suggesting that they were now ready to receive a deed of the property he had so generously bestowed upon them. Christopher Scott did not like this very well; anyway, he thought it was time they did something for themselves; so he told them they could have the deed when they raised the money for a manse. This was rather awkward, as times were hard and the expenses of the church were about all they could manage. So Christopher Scott went to Scotland, leaving a note behind to tell them what he thought of them.

After a long time, Christopher Scott came back, rather silent and a bit morose, and very difficult to talk to. There is a legend that says he one day locked up the Kirk, put the key in his pocket and went away, but returned again, bringing with him a dove with an olive branch in its mouth, as a sign of peace. If this incident happened, it was evidently deemed best not to record it, but there is the dove with the olive branch spreading its brazen wings over the pulpit. There it has been for the last hundred years, and there it is to-day, and that is the story of the Kirk and Christopher Scott.

The Roman Catholics were the next to build a church, about the year 1825. This old building stood at the further end of the town, on the corner of Parr and Mary Streets, Mr. John Dunn having given the land for the purpose. The first Mass was celebrated on Christmas Day, 1821, at the house of Mr. Henry O'Neil, shortly after the family arrived in this country. The house, now known as the Anchorage, was occupied by the priest in those early days. In 1885 the present beautiful little church was built on King Street, nearer the centre of the town.

The Methodist Church was built about the year 1831, with the Rev. Henry Daniel for its first minister.

The Baptist church was organized about the year 1865, by the Rev. T. W. Crawley. It was known as the second Baptist Church. The little building at Bayside, with its interesting old doorway, holds the honour of being the first Baptist Church and is well past its hundredth year.

10 THE YEARS OF PEACE

HENRY GOLDSMITH, a nephew of the poet Oliver Goldsmith, drifted into St. Andrews about the year 1800, or possibly some time before. He was a poet himself in a small way and was as charming, visionary, and unpractical as any poet needs to be.

There is a little stream that crosses the road near Gilman's Corner, on the way to St. Stephen, still known as Goldsmith's Stream. It is the outlet of Bartlett's mill stream. In the early days the country all around this stream was thickly wooded with enormous trees. Here Henry Goldsmith had visions of saw mills and lumbering operations and wheels turned by this same stream, thus he would fill his pockets with gold. He built a small shack beside it and removed there with his wife and children. There was no road in those days, the only access to the place was by water. Goldsmith's visions haunted him, and he must go back to England and tell the people there about the wealth of woodlands in this country and about the stream that was waiting to turn the wheels. He would form a company to exploit the resources of this wonderful place and so to England he went, leaving his unfortunate wife and their six small children alone in the shack by the side of the stream. He thought he had left her provided for—he had left her food and a little money. The food in time became exhausted and the money was unavailing in that lonely spot. The children found wild berries and she dug clams for them on the shore. She was a delicate and gentle lady. She had been accustomed to comfort and luxury in Providence, waited on by servants, and unaccustomed to work. She had never even had to brush her own hair till she married her visionary husband. Now she could only beg food and assistance from the Indians, who occasionally passed that way. She realized the autumn was fast approaching; she saw no chance of escape—she was in despair.

One morning, while down on the clam flats at low tide, she saw afar someone coming along the shore on horseback. Was it friend or foe? She watched the approaching stranger with both fear and hope. As the figure came nearer she beheld a little woman cantering along the shore with a large hamper strapped behind her. It was Mehetible Calef. An Indian had told her about the lovely lady who dug clams every day to feed her children. She had ridden up along the shore from St. Andrews, while the tide was out, to see for herself if the Indian's tale was true.

That was a joyful day for the Goldsmith family. When the hamper was opened it contained such food as they had not seen for many a long day—bread and butter, milk and eggs, ham and chicken, and apples and cakes. What a sight for six hungry children and a despairing mother!

The little lady stayed and talked with them till the tide came up close to the shore, and, when it turned, she mounted her horse again and started for home, leaving the hamper and the remainder of its contents behind her. She promised that she would send up some men in a boat to bring them all down to St. Andrews. And down they all came in the boat next day and were the guests of Mehetible Calef for the next six months. Then the visionary husband returned from a somewhat unsuccessful trip to England. It must have been a lively household for Mehetible Calef with a large family of her own to care for as well.

The Goldsmiths must have stayed on in St. Andrews for some time. We find a reference to the Goldsmith house in 1810, and Goldsmith seems to have been at one time connected with the Custom House. We also find him visiting Ward Chipman, in Saint John, and suffering with the gout *"feeling the comfort of one of Chipman's arm chairs," and with both feet "Raised on a Cuishing." In this distressing situation he writes to Edward Winslow for the loan of a bottle of medicinal water to relieve his sufferings.

The Goldsmith family finally moved to Nova Scotia where the son, Oliver, became famous as a poet. He published a slim book of poems entitled *The Rising Village and Other Poems.* This was the first book of poems to be published by a native of Canada. As Oliver was born in St. Andrews, this is recorded on a tablet placed on the doorway of the Post Office.

St. Andrews was by this time enjoying a pleasant social life. It was the custom to give a grand ball on the 4th of June, the birthday of the old King. We hear of the ladies tying paper over the white lilac trees, lest they should bloom too early for this festive occasion. Slender ladies in short-waisted dresses and long narrow skirts, their hair piled high on graceful heads, fastened with a tortoise-shell comb, all grouped about a white

---

lilac bush on a June day, a picture for Kate Greenaway, and so "long live our gracious King!" they said. Just one month later, across that disputed little river and down the bay, at the town of Eastport, another celebration would take place with loud and vociferous patriotism, decrying this same gracious King as the most cruel and terrible of all cruel tyrants known to history. And far away across the sea the old King in his great castle at Windsor was slowly sinking to a tragic old age, playing the harpsichord and weeping for the wrongs of his Britannic Majesty's loyal subjects in North America, while his gay, handsome, irresponsible son acted as Regent. Those were strange and interesting times.

To these balls would flock such people of note as members of Admiral Owen's household, and Captain Farrell from Deer Island. This courtly old gentleman, who still loved to dance, was a great friend of Dr. Calef's; they were the last two that wore the three-cornered hats in St. Andrews. Younger men considered them old-fashioned and had adopted the narrow rimmed bell-shaped beaver. When Captain Farrell came to town, and Dr. Calef met him on the street, both old gentlemen would remove their three-cornered hats with a flourish and make a profound bow, hand on heart. The one would say, "Be covered, Sir," and the other would protest, "Not before you, Sir," and so these two gallant old courtiers would bow themselves up half the length of the Front Street.

Another pretty scene in those days sometimes occurred at the jail brook. This brook, that once ran through forests primeval, crossed all the parallel streets of the town, from the back of the present jail, down the steep hill leading to the old post office and out to the sea. It has long since been piped below the surface, but in those days it was crossed by stepping stones. The ladies in their long, tight skirts found crossing this stream very difficult and would stand waiting on the brink till some gallant gentlemen came to carry them over.

The gentlemen of the town formed a club, known as the Friendly Society. This met every week at the homes of the different members, where they enjoyed pleasant social intercourse and discussed some special problem that the members suggested; the subjects were many and varied, judging from the old minute book. Spirits and water were the only refreshments allowed. They used to meet on Saturday nights, but Dr. Calef did not approve of this. The old Doctor had Puritan views about the Sabbath, and Saturday night should be spent in solemn preparation. So the night of meeting was changed to Friday.

One evening Mr. Jack chose for a subject: "Is a knowledge of the dead languages absolutely necessary in what are called the learned professions?"

Another evening Mr. Pagan brought up the question: "Is a person whose disposition is to resent supposed injuries, or one who submits to real ones, the best member of society?"

Colonel Wyer on another occasion wanted to know: "In what manner female education may be made to contribute to rendering them better."

Mr. Elisha Andrews (a son of the good old parson) propounded a religious problem: "How far will an observance of the precepts of morality insure the salvation of those who know nothing of a future state, but from the light of nature?"

Mr. McLauchlan wanted to know: "How could Samson catch three hundred foxes so soon, when he sent them with firebrands to burn the corn of the Philistines?"

One night Mr. Pagan asked, just by way of getting down to practical subjects: "Whether it is best to prune fruit trees in the autumn or the spring?"

Unfortunately, the old minute book does not tell us what conclusions were arrived at in answering these questions.

We were told that Parson Andrews was the organizer and leader of the Friendly Society and that after his death it declined, but it must have revived again, for we find the record books of an old St. Andrews Friendly Society that dates back to 1866.

11   WAR AGAIN

UPON such peaceful scenes as these arose the war clouds of 1812. They watched them gathering with much concern in the little Loyalist town, so lately settled down to enjoy its years of peace.

New England did not want war either, and said so quite plainly; it even put the flags at half-mast in Boston harbour the day that war was declared. But the young Republic had its own army now, and its navy too, and was looking about for more worlds to conquer and more grievances from British Tyrants. President Madison had visions and dreams of ruling the whole of North America, and the people were so convinced now that tyranny was the sole aim and object of all British rule, that they were certain His Britannic Majesty's loyal subjects in North America would be glad to make a change, if they could find the slightest opportunity for doing so.

The Governor-General, Sir George Prevost, had at the instigation of his officious secretary, Ryland, sent a man named Henry to travel through the States and act as a secret agent to discover the temper and sentiment of the American people. Henry was not satisfied with the pay offered for this job and went to England, hoping to find a more profitable market for his information. Over in poor distracted Europe, Napoleon everywhere used his far-reaching influence to fan the flames of war. One of his secret agents, falling in with Henry, completely hoodwinked him, lured him to Washington, and with the persuasive manner of a French courtier induced the authorities at Washington to purchase all Henry's secret correspondence with Ryland. All the cruel, tyrannical, unkind things that Mr. Ryland ever said when he wrote to Mr. Henry, were worth at least fifty thousand dollars, which Mr. Munroe gladly paid for them. Direct evidence of British tyranny was evidently very scarce and expensive in those days. Poor Mr. Henry spent the whole fifty thousand in buying the French gentleman's family estate in France, which happened to be up for sale at the time, but when he went to France, armed with the deed, he found there wasn't any estate there.

However, Napoleon thought America had better declare war on England, and that was one of his plans that worked out very well, and Madison thought so too, so between the "right of search" and the Ryland letters the war was begun.

Those were trying times everywhere. What with embargoes and Orders-in-Council, and decrees about neutrals and non-combatants, and nations making war or peace at a minute's notice, and no telegraphs or telephones in those days, how in the world were vessels to know where they should go, or who they belonged to? And England had fixed ideas about the duty of neutrals in the matter of deserters, and the Americans held fixed ideas about the "right of search," and President Madison wanted war, and Napoleon wanted war, and so it did not matter much whether New England and Canada wanted it or not, there was war.

Then General Hull crossed the border at Detroit, proclaiming loudly that he had come to save poor dear Canada from "tyranny and oppression." He would just bring the American flag over to the other side of the Great Lakes and every one would be happy ever afterwards. But everyone seemed to like "British tyranny" on the other side of the border, and the Loyalists who had settled in Upper Canada said they much preferred it to the "Liberty, Fraternity and Equality" that had been handed out to them when they left the States, and so General Hull had to make the best of it and take what was handed out to him, though undoubtedly he was unprepared for the surprise.

All this time St. Andrews was quite uneasy. There it was, right on the border and on the most exposed point of the frontier. The men of the town briskly started drilling on the Barrack Hill and ships of war patrolled the harbour. A very wise agreement was made between the people living on both sides of the St. Croix River. They held various meetings at both sides of the border, and Eastport and St. Andrews vowed to each other that no matter what happened they would, if possible, avoid bloodshed or open hostility, and this compact was faithfully adhered to by both sides through the whole period of the war.

Nevertheless, St. Andrews prepared for war; three block houses were erected: one at Indian Point, one at Joe's Point and one halfway between the other two, by the red rocks at the head of the town. A barracks was also built and St. Andrews became a garrisoned town. But no blood was shed along the banks of the St. Croix River.

The chief grievances of the Americans had been against the British navy, but they staged the war along the shores of the Great Lakes as far out of reach of the British navy as possible.

Canada had done nothing to bring about the war and was in no way responsible for it, but she was obliged to bear the greater part of the burden. England was at that time entering upon her last struggle with Napoleon and could ill spare troops and supplies. New Brunswick sent a regiment to Quebec, the famous

104th, who marched the entire distance on snow shoes in the month of February, 1813.

At this time we again hear of Mehetible Calef. She was a widow now, the Captain having died at sea, and her father, the good old doctor, was dead also. Her older sons had decided, at the outbreak of the war, it would be safer to build a house farther out in the country on wild lands owned by their father, where they had now cleared land for a farm and had already built a barn.

One night, when the house was completed, Mehetible was staying there with her oldest son. During his absence to the town on an errand, five American soldiers appeared at the door demanding food and a night's lodging. She gave them food and then, providing them with quilts and blankets, told them they could sleep in the barn. Her courage and gentle courtesy impressed the men and they went off peacefully enough. When her son returned she had retired to bed, leaving the door unlocked. She called down to him to be sure and bolt the door, but said nothing of the soldiers in the barn, knowing that the hot-headed youth would never allow shelter to the enemies of his country and that it would be dangerous for him to get into any kind of dispute with five armed soldiers, with whom his country was at war, so she bravely kept her secret until he finally discovered the blankets in the barn where the soldiers had left them.

Meanwhile, news came at long intervals from the seat of war, alternating tales of loss and victory. Those were anxious days. They were prosperous days, too. The Quoddy Islands were a Mecca for smugglers.

Many of these islands were disputed territory, and almost any islands along the coast were able to claim nationality of either country at a moment's notice, according to requirements of goods found on them. The St. Andrews merchants profited richly.

Eastport at this time was put under martial law by the British, who claimed that Moose Island, on which the town of Eastport stands, was one of the islands mentioned in the treaty as being on British territory. The people of Eastport very wisely submitted and were quite surprised to find themselves treated with kindness and consideration and extremely well governed. The clock-work regularity and perfect system of the British occupation made a lasting impression on the inhabitants.

Sir Thomas Hardy was in command during the first year, the same Hardy so well known in history as the friend of Nelson.

The British officers lived in lavish style, and the inhabitants of Eastport found a ready market for their produce to supply banquets of the officers' mess. The officers also established a theatre, where they gave private theatricals on a most elaborate scale. The inhabitants could not leave the place without a permit, which must have been somewhat irksome. However, permits were easily obtained and never denied, without some important reason and they submitted very sensibly to this decree. Now one of these permits is treasured as a precious curio.

When the troops were finally withdrawn, after an occupation of four years, they were presented with gifts and testimonials of respect by the people. That same year Sir John Coape Sherbrooke sailed down the coast and captured Penobscot which, for the second time, fell into the possession of the British, and into Halifax harbour sailed the *Shannon,* leading the captive *Chesapeak.*

In Upper Canada and on the Great Lakes the war waged fiercely. The gallant Brock had sacrificed his life in gaining Queenston Heights, and the inadequate fleet on the Great Lakes had met with sad reverses. Tecumseh, the stout old Indian ally, had been slain. There was much privation and suffering and destruction in Canada, but the little town of St. Andrews remained peaceful as when the Loyalists first came to it.

Finally on Christmas Eve, 1814, when little Loyalist children were hanging up their stockings, the treaty of peace was signed at Ghent. All lands and prisoners captured had to be returned on either side, and nothing was said about the right of search or the Ryland letters, and nothing was gained for anyone, but some very useful experience. Both sides were very thankful that the war was over, though they did not get the news till three months after the treaty was signed.

12   THE SUCCEEDING RACE

THE prosperity of the merchants during the war of 1812 continued through the years of peace. They seem to have dealt in a large variety of goods. They sent their vessels to many ports and they returned with cargoes of any sort of merchandise that could be readily disposed of. This is shown in an account of Christopher Scott, rendered to Mehetible Calef, written in the finest copper-plate handwriting, and containing some of the following items:

3¼ yds. cassimere	16/-.
1 pr. gloves	3/-.
1 lb. nails	8d.
275 ft. boards	40/-.
¼ gal. wine	2/6.
½ gal. rum	3/-.
1 bbl. flour	17/6.
16 panes glass	10/-.

Another account is from Hugh Leash, the tailor, and shows the prices of those days.

To making a pair of panteloons	7/-.
” ” ” ” small clothes	8/-.
” ” a waist-coat	6/6.
” ” a long coat	17/6.
” ” a pr. gaters	4/6.
” 2 skanes of thread	5d.

Shipbuilding was carried on extensively at that time in St. Andrews, also at St. Stephen, Beaver Harbour, Campobello and Gand Manan. Agriculture, lumbering and fishing all prospered and found a ready market.

The Battle of Waterloo had ended the long struggle with Napoleon, who was now landed safely in St. Helena out of harm's way, and the motherland was at peace at last.

Many of the old Loyalists had passed away and others had come to take their places in public affairs. Dr. Frye had succeeded Dr. Calef, and was later followed by Dr. McStay and Dr. Gove.

Colin Campbell, Jr., succeeded Elisha Andrews as Sheriff and was later succeeded by Sheriff Thomas Jones.

Harris Hatch, son of old Colonel Christopher Hatch, was made Judge of Probate and Mr. John Dunn had been superannuated. The Collector of Customs was Captain J. M. Spearman.

Mr. James Berry kept a private school where he instructed the youth of the town at the rate of ten shillings a quarter and eight shillings for the younger boys.

There was another school for younger children on the outskirts of the town, kept by a curious old gentleman named McCarthy. Besides tuition fees, every family whose children attended this school, was expected to supply a cord of wood for fuel in winter. There were no holidays, winter or summer, but on Christmas day the boys arrived early and barred the door on the master in order to secure this one day for a holiday. It was a regular, traditional ceremony, and the master made very little resistance, but had to make his appearance.

In the year 1818, the County Grammar School was built, and this was a great step in educational advancement. It was not entirely a free school, but the government voted some funds for its erection and support.

Mr. John Cassils, a presbyterian minister, who had come out from Scotland to teach in King's College, Windsor, was the first master of the Grammar School. He was a gentleman of keen intellect and great learning, and seems to have been greatly respected in the community. He frequently assisted in the services of the Kirk. One of his daughters married Robert Cockburn, and their descendants still live in St. Andrews.

Mr. Cassils was succeeded by Mr. D. S. Morrison, who, to distinguish him from all the other Morrisons in town, was nicknamed 'Long Morrison.'

Later it was taught by the curate of the English Church. Mr. Ranald Smith, Mr. C. M. Sills and Mr. Partridge (afterwards Dean of the Cathedral at Fredericton) all taught in the Grammar School, while assisting the Rector of All Saints Church.

The first directors of the school were the Rector of the parish, together with Robert Pagan, John Campbell, John Dunn, Colin Campbell, David W. Jack, Harris Hatch, Thomas Wyer, Jr., and John Strang. The little wooden building remained in use for over a century. The St. Andrews people were very proud of their Grammar School. As one generation after another passed through its doors, they could find initials of their grandparents carved on the ancient desks and benches. No building ever called forth more sentiment and affection than did that little wooden school-house. After the introduction of free schools, it was used for the High School grades, and was abandoned when the present concrete school-house was erected. The old Grammar School building was destroyed by the same disastrous fire that burned the old Coffee House.

Some years later the Court House was built and the massive stone jail beside it, with a secluded yard for the purpose of hanging criminals.

The first newspaper was the *St. Andrews Herald*, published by Mr. Stubbs. It was succeeded by the *Standard,* published by Mr. George Smith, and kept on for nearly half a century by his son, Mr. Adam Smith. *The Bay Pilot* followed the *Standard,* with Mr. John S. Magee as editor, and after that the *Beacon,* edited by Mr. R. E. Armstrong, and later by Mr. Broad.

An interesting character in the early days was Mr. Joseph Walton. He was of pre-Loyalist stock and was the first owner of that beautiful estate now owned by Senator Cairine Wilson. Old Mr. Walton, besides being a successful farmer, also composed poetry at times. His verses were remarkable for a somewhat extraordinary capacity for rhyming, such as

> The first of March
> All hearts doth sarch.
> The hay is very scanty
> And the cattle very wanty.

He was a very kindly old gentleman as well as a poet, and brought up a large family; when they were grown up he built a large white house on the top of the hill so that they would have plenty of room to dance in. His wife was an invalid for some years, and Mr. Walton took the best of care of her; he even excused himself in the middle of a dinner, given by the Agricultural Society, saying it was time for him to go home and put Mrs. Walton to bed. After his death, the family drifted away and the place was eventually sold to Dr. Tupper, afterwards Sir Charles Tupper.

Captain John Mowat, cousin to Captain Henry of Falmouth fame, having retired from the sea, now settled down at St. Andrews. He had married a beautiful Jewess during his travels around the world, one Rachel Abrahams, of whom it has been said she was "an Israelite indeed, in whom there was no guile." He had been commander of the Duke of Kent's ship the *Princess Amelia,* and had had many interesting experiences both on land and sea. A really beautiful little poem was written to commemorate his passing, which still remains, though the name of the author is unknown.

Oh fare-thee-well, Mowat, the morning may bloom
And shed its first soft dewy light on thy tomb.
But its ray shall ne'er call back thy spirit that's fled,
Nor wake the cold corpse from the trance of the dead.
I have seen thee in sickness, have known thee in health,
Surrounded by honour, by beauty, and wealth,
When our loved Royal Edward, young, gallant and brave
Committed his life to thy care on the wave.
I have marked, when these splendours extraneous were flown,
With pleasure, the virtues all purely thine own.
Then fare-thee-well, Mowat, from earth thou art gone,
Yet thy memory shall live in my bosom alone,
And when life is receding, my last prayer shall be,
To meet you in Heaven and repose there with thee.

The old Captain left a son, John, who also followed the sea and finally settled down to end his days at Bayside. He answered to the roistering nickname of 'Hurricane Jack.' St. Andrews seems to have had a real genius for nicknames in the old days.

Most interesting of all the colourful figures on that fading tapestry, is Mr. Charles Joseph Briscoe; always seen riding through the town, with royal dignity, on his great white horse. He hinted darkly that he was closely connected with royalty, but it was a secret he would never disclose, though he had papers to prove it, so he said, and some day the truth would be revealed to the people of St. Andrews, but not till long after he was dead and gone. His job at that time was 'tide waiter' and 'searcher' for the port of St. Andrews; he had held a similar important post at Gravesend before he left England. Not a very regal position for one of the blood royal, but he seems to have received funds from some mysterious source which enabled him to keep up a dignified appearance in his household. A note of invitation has come down to us, most prim and decorous. It reads:

Dear Miss ....:
          I intend having a small party this evening, duly matronized of course, and it will afford me much pleasure if you and your sister and brother will honour it with your presence at 1/2 past eight.
          Sincerely
Monday Mg.   C. BRISCOE.

As the note is undated, it may have been written in later years by his son, also Charles Briscoe. That was an age of much formality even for the younger generation.

When Charles Joseph Briscoe came to his last days, he left directions that the packet of papers that would prove his royal birth should be buried with him and that, after fifty years had elapsed, his grave was to be opened and the letters taken out and read, and the facts given to the St. Andrews public. He gave minute details for this ceremony, mentioning those who were to be in attendance. Dr. Gove was among those present; also Dr. Ketchum, the Rector of the Parish at the time. Alas, when the years were accomplished and the papers recovered, they were so moulded as to be completely illegible. The only thing among them in a state of preservation was an ivory miniature of George IV. It is currently supposed that the old gentleman was a son of this monarch and Mrs. Fitz-Herbert, to whom he was secretly married in London. The miniature was set with pearls and a lock of hair was set in the back.

Mrs. Briscoe kept a girls' school for some years after her husband's death, and thus supported her two children.

The old fire brigade, or 'Heart and Hand Society', was organized to protect the town from fire. Each member owned a couple of light papier-mâché buckets, with his name printed on them; these were kept in the front hall, and they would seize them at the first alarm of fire. All the men of the town would form a bucket brigade from the nearest well to the scene of the fire.

An old rhyme composed when this Society was started, is still remembered and is interesting in the old names it commemorates. It was remembered for generations, and each succeeding generation seems to have added names to it that had any possibility of rhyme.

"The town's on fire"
Said Colonel Wyer.
"Is it indeed"
Said Mr. Seed.
"Where, where"
Said Mr. Blair.
"At Katy's Cove"
Said Dr. Gove.
"Run, run"
Said Mr. Dunn.
"I can run no faster"
Said Mr. McMaster.
"No need to cry"
Said Dr. Frye.
"How did it catch"
Said Colonel Hatch.

and so on through endless verses.

A man by the name of McIntosh owned a large amount of land below the Barrack Hill, sloping down to the Cove. He left this to his daughter Katy, who was a very 'masterful woman', and the terror of young boys who came to swim in the Cove. That is how Katy's Cove got its name.

The Barrack Hill is also noted for the fact that a woman, named Mrs. Bean, was buried alive there. She suffered from a distressing skin disease, probably eczema, and was recommended to remain buried in the earth for twenty-four hours; this rather severe treatment she consented to try, so they dug a hole and buried her, all but the head. Her chief fear seems to have been dogs, so they left a boy to watch her and drive off too inquisitive dogs. The boy grew tired of the job and ran away. Passers-by were amazed to see a woman's head, in a large coal-scuttle bonnet, apparently growing out of the ground and quickly turning from side to side in search of dogs. It is unfortunate that history does not tell us whether or not Mrs. Bean was cured of her malady.

13 SOCIAL LIFE

THE garrison stationed in St. Andrews at this time gave much gaiety and colour to the social life of the town, and people able to retire with private means found it a pleasant place to live in, and drifted there to end their days. We still hear of balls being given. The following poem, written in 1826, gives a quaint description of one of these festivities:

THE BACHELORS' BALL

St Andrews, Valentine's Day, 1826

The clock strikes eight and we repair
With hearts devoid of grief and care,
To yonder gay and brilliant Hall,
With joy to hail the Bachelors' Ball;
And now assembled in the room,
Where Hope presides in Beauty's bloom,
See! with delight each beau repair
To single out his favourite Fair!

McMaster first, with joyous face,
Delighted, shows each nymph her place;
While one, prized far above the rest,
Triumphant reigns within his breast.
Next Street appears; but, stop my pen!
Our every thought of him is vain,
For, he too, owns a fair one's sway
And we must look another way.

The next is graceful Garnet seen,
With crimson badge and pensive mien,
That gem so costly and so rare
So highly prized by every fair.
Rodgers, for taste and judgment famed,
At whom the brightest eyes are aimed,
But aimed in vain; his flighty heart
Resists the power of Cupid's dart.
Now Campbell comes to take his part,
Delight of every lady's heart;
His form symmetrical excels
In contra dances and quadrills.
So graceful, easy and so free,
O! he's the very man for me.
Our grateful tribute now is due
To the Master, modest, kind and true,
Who freely shares the general mirth,
Wholly unconscious of his worth.
McLachlan comes skilled in each art
To win the proudest fair one's heart.
All must confess his powers to please,
More hearts than one he's robbed of ease.
Now, last among the swains, is seen
The gentle and the good McKean.
Each belle his kind attention shares
And grateful smiles repay his cares.
Promotors of the festive throng,
To each and all—our thanks belong;
Accept our best and warmest praise,
In these our simple, humble lays.
Now may sweet Hope her blessings shower
And lead you soon to Hymen's bower;
Secure from miseries of this life—
By Heaven's best gift—a loving wife.

Between the years 1830-1840, many new families
had come to St. Andrews. Also throughout the
country, to the farmers living on the old grants, there
came from England 'remittance men'. Charlotte
County in the old days seems to have been a haven

for the black sheep of the English gentry. They were not as black as they were painted, many of them; they were misfits in England, one can well believe, but chiefly because they were bored with a life of elegance and ease; they wanted to work with their hands, to live in wild, open country and to choose their friends among simple, honest, unpretentious people. All this they found in the land of their adoption. Most of them settled down on farms of their own; the remittance from home was a great help and they never tried to force on the community the manners and customs of their former home. They were thoroughbreds and they left their impress, for to them may be given some of the credit for the gentle manners and soft voices found in so many remote homes throughout the country. Such names as Caven, Mears, Simpson, and many others, can be recalled in this connection.

A curious document or indenture of apprenticeship comes down to us from this period, which is worth noting, as it shows the exacting servitude required of an apprentice and seems like a cross between slavery and adoption. However, we are told in this case 'little Jimmy' was so kindly treated in his master's family that one of the neighbours complained that he was dressed too much like a gentleman and it would lead other apprentices to expect the same treatment:

"This indenture witnesseth that Robert Lindsay, of the Parish of Burton, County of Sunbury and Province of New Brunswick, labourer, of the one part hath bound his infant son James, who is now at this time two years and three months old, as an apprentice to Nathaniel Hubbard of the Parish, County and Province aforesaid, and to his heirs And assigns of the other part, to learn the art, Trade and Mystery of Farming and after the manner of an apprentice to serve from the day of the date hereof until he shall arrive at the age of twenty-one years of age, During all which time of servitude the said apprentice his master faithfully shall serve, his secrets keep, his lawful commands every where readily obey; He shall do no damage to his said master, nor see it done by others without letting or giving notice thereof to his said master; He shall not waste his said Master's goods, nor lend them unlawfully to any person or persons. He shall not commit fornication nor contract matrimony within the said time as above mentioned. At cards, dice or any other unlawful game he shall not play whereby his said Master may have damage, with his own goods, nor the goods of others, without license from his said Master he shall neither buy nor sell. He shall not absent himself day or night from his said Master's service without his leave, nor haunt ale houses, taverns or play houses; but in all things behave himself as a faithful apprentice ought to do during the said term, and the said Master shall use the utmost of his endeavour to teach or cause to be taught or instructed the said apprentice in the art, trade or mystery of Farming and provide for him sufficient meat, drink, apparel, lodging and washing, fitting for an apprentice during the said term which is until he is twenty-one years old. And the aforesaid Nathaniel Hubbard on his part doth agree to teach or cause him to be taught, and instructed to cypher, read and write, and at the expiration of the said term when he is twenty-one years old, the said Nathaniel Hubbard or his heirs and assigns shall give unto the said apprentice one yoke of steers rising three years old, and two suits of wearing apparel, one suitable for the Sabbath and the other for working days—and for the true performance of all and singular and covenants and agreements aforesaid the said parties bind themselves each unto the other firmly by these presents.

In Witness whereof the said Parties have interchangeably set their hand and seals hereunto, the 24th day of November in the year of our Lord one thousand eight hundred and forty nine. (1849).

Signed, sealed and delivered
in the presence of

WM. J. GILBERT.   ROBERT LINDSAY.
H. L. HUBBARD.   NATHE. HUBBARD.

Unfortunately, little Jimmy did not live to enjoy the yoke of steers and the two suits of wearing apparel, for he died at the age of eight, deeply lamented by the family.

Roads had now been made through the province and stage coaches came from Saint John and Fredericton. It was always an exciting moment when the coach arrived, tooting its horn at the head of the town and driving at a gallop to the Market Square, with its load of passengers.

Speaking of roads, an interesting item appears in an old letter, complaining that as soon as good roads were built in the province "the young people would all want to drive in wheeled vehicles and forget the use of their legs". Those were the days when a man walked ten miles to the mill with a sack of grain on his back.

There was a delightful little tavern at Bocabec, where the stage coach stopped to exchange horses and which is still known as the 'Old Exchange'. There, in old days, sleighing parties would go from St. Andrews, engage a country fiddler and spend the evening dancing.

Much activity centred in Chamcook, where Mr. John Wilson had started many thriving mills. It was a perfect hive of industry, with saw mills, grist mills, a paper mill (the first in Canada) and shipbuilding on a most extensive scale. Most prominent in the shipbuilding at this time were the Townsend family. Robert Townsend, an expert shipbuilder, came out from England and, with his sons, carried on this important industry for many years.

Squire Wilson, as they called him, lived in a large stone house, set in a lovely beech wood. He wanted Chamcook to be as much like an English village as possible, and his house to be like an English manor, surrounded by a deer park. He stocked the beech wood with deer, but one of them inconsiderately gored a woman, and the deer became unpopular; but the park remained.

The house was a charming place, and there the Squire and his lady dispensed a royal hospitality. Memories of those old Chamcook parties still linger in story and legend. The Squire's lady, always sweet and placid and a perfect hostess, played for the dances with much dash and spirit; as she played she sang, *The Campbells are Coming* or *Old Dan Tucker*. They danced the lancers in those days, the polka and mazurka, and always ended with *Sir Roger*. Very stately couples, the gentlemen with their high stock collars and tightly buttoned coats; the ladies with full skirts and sloping shoulders, hair in ringlets, three little curls on either side of high, white foreheads. There would be officers there, too, in scarlet and gold braid.

It is told of the Squire, that one day while riding through the country, he stopped at the 'Old Exchange' for a drink and the landlord's pretty little wife brought out to him a mug of beer, for which he rewarded her with a kiss, as any good old Squire would be expected to do under similar circumstances. Next morning, while the Wilson family were having breakfast with their guests, an irate landlord, with a large horsewhip, thundered into the room. He turned to Mrs. Wilson and announced "Madam, I have come here to tell you that your husband kissed my wife." The placid lady was quite unruffled and said soothingly "Then you come here and kiss me and we will call it square." The outraged husband was pacified, though he did not avail himself of the invitation.

Among the members of the Squire's household was a little orphan girl named Lucy Sprague. Mrs. Wilson had brought her up from childhood, and the mantle of her mistress seems in a measure to have descended to her. In later life we hear of her keeping house in St. Andrews for Mr. Wilson's brother, Edward, in a pretty little red brick cottage on the hill, with honeysuckle beside the door. She outlived this old gentleman, who left her the house and for many years she kept boarders there, in fact, Miss Sprague's boarding house is still remembered. Her vivacious wit, her old furniture, her bountiful table, and her unlimited fund of old stories, made her house a delightful place at which to stay. She lived to a great age and always spoke of the Wilson family with unfailing love and respect.

Squire Wilson built the beautiful little stone church at Chamcook, which added greatly to the English effect.

The Squire's enterprises seem to have been extremely prosperous. He had a number of vessels sailing the seas, carrying the product of his mills to many distant ports. The *Lady of the Lake,* the *Silver Waves,* the *Pilgrim,* and many others were known as the ships of Squire Wilson.

The *Pilgrim* was wrecked and this tragedy afterwards figured in a famous libel suit between Mr. Spearman of the Custom House and the Squire; the contention being that the *Pilgrim* was wrecked for the insurance.

Mr. Spearman seems to have been over-scrupulous in enforcing the customs laws, and made himself so unpopular with the merchants of the town that they sent a petition to the House of Assembly to have him removed from office.

The Government, having referred the matter, with the list of petitioners, to Mr. Spearman, he returned it with his opinions affixed. This list has been preserved at the Custom House and, we hope, is a somewhat prejudiced account, especially in the case of Christopher Scott. It bears the date 21st June, 1831.

A Report of the Collector of St. Andrews
on the Character of the Memorialists:

Christopher Scott.—Merchant and ship-owner. Mr. Scott is almost constantly in a state of intoxication. He was absent in England during the investigation, but his brother, son, and nephew who conduct his business, declare that they know of no cause of complaint.

William Hunt, M.D.—This person does not reside here, he is a travelling apothecary and has never, to our knowledge, transacted any business at this office.

Joseph Walton.—Is a small farmer in this neighborhood, formerly a shipbuilder and smuggler.

Gordon Gilchrist.—Is by trade a carpenter.

Alexander McDowell.—Is a small farmer, but lately arrived from Scotland.

Edward Wilson.—Was, until lately, a clerk in the employ of his brother John Wilson, the principal mover in getting up this petition. He is now in business for himself as a store-keeper.

William Ker, Merchant—Is an auctioneer and shopkeeper. We never heard of him as a merchant before he brought forward his complaint on the present assertion.

Ebenezer Sweet.—Merchant and ship-owner, has lately arrived from Nova Scotia, where his ship is registered.

Francis Jones.—Merchant and ship-owner, is a fraudulent bankrupt, residing in the United States and a notorious smuggler.

Joseph Wilson.—The remarks opposite his brother Edward Wilson, with whom he is in partnership, applies equally.

William Babcock, Merchant.—Is a tavern-keeper.

Thomas Wyer, Jr., J.P. and agent for Lloyds.—Loads a ship occasionally.

John Wilson, J.P.—Was the instigator and principal mover in getting up this petition. He is a notorious smuggler; see the case of the Brig. "John".

C. R. Hatheway, J.P.—We know nothing of Mr. Hatheway except that he occasionally imports a barrel of flour for his own use.

John McMaster—Merchant and ship-owner, is the junior partner of the firm of Allanshaw and McMaster. Mr. Allanshaw, the Chairman of the Chamber of Commerce, gave evidence in our favour.

James Campbell, Merchant and ship-owner, is the junior partner in the firm of Ker and Campbell.

William Chandler, gentleman—Attorney at Law.

Edwin Todd, Merchant—was lately junior partner of the firm of Francis Jones & Co.

L. H. Whitlock, Merchant—Is a store-keeper and auctioneer.

Donald Morrison, Provision Dealer.—Was formerly a carpenter and now a butcher.

James Parkinson, Merchant.—Is a baker and retail grocer and is a most notorious smuggler.

Whatever the truth may be, this gives us a very representative list of the men who were actively engaged in business at that time in St. Andrews; but the comments were evidently written with a venomous pen.

The petition and venomous remarks on both sides finally ended in a law-suit, in which Mr. Spearman sued Squire Wilson for libel, accused him of smuggling and wrecking the *Pilgrim* for the insurance. Mr. Wilson in return accused Mr. Spearman of everything under the sun that an unpopular customs house officer could be accused of, and Colonel Wyer almost got mixed up in a duel. All the leading merchants went up to Fredericton to hear the case tried, and after four or five days sitting, the court decided to give Mr. Spearman a shilling for damages.

The lawyer for the defence in Squire Wilson's lawsuit was the Honourable Neville Parker, afterwards Master of the Rolls at Fredericton. In later years he moved to St. Andrews and purchased the brick house formerly owned by Dr. Frye, opposite the English church. The family lived there for many years.

There were two children in the Wilson family, a daughter Susan, who afterwards married Dr. William Bayard of Saint John; and a son Thomas, who married Miss Howe, a relative of the Honourable Joseph Howe of Nova Scotia.

A mysterious gentleman, by the name of Mc-Laughlan, appeared in Chamcook about this time and built a house on the side of the mountain. This house was supposed to be haunted, and for many years remained vacant. A tragic story is told of the house-keeper, who, on a very cold night when her master was away, piled up the logs on the huge fireplace and lay down on the hearth rug to await his return. She fell asleep and the logs blazed into such a tremendous fire that she was roasted to death in front of them.

101

This tragedy seems to have so distressed Mr. McLaughlan that he abandoned the place and was heard of no more.

The Squire's son occupied the house for a time after his marriage, but the doors opened mysteriously and strange unaccountable footsteps were heard through the corridors, and they too abandoned the place.

Years after, one of the Townsend family bought it, tore down the old haunted house and built a more modern dwelling in its place.

This has now become the beautiful estate known as 'Rossmont'.

14 BORDER TROUBLES

IN THE year 1837 there was again trouble along the border. Poor old George III had long since gone to his reward. His sons, who succeeded him, had likewise passed on, and in this year of grace we hear of the little princess Victoria .tripping down stairs, on the dawn of a June morning, to meet the Archbishop of Canterbury and the Lord Chamberlain; and to learn that she was now Queen of England. It was August before the news reached New Brunswick, and the *Royal Gazette,* published at Fredericton, came out with columns deep-lined in black for the death of old King William. Major-General Harvey, Lieutenant-Governor and Commander-in-Chief of the Province, issued any number of proclamations, and in St.

Andrews they made a great celebration for the coronation, and roasted an ox in the market square and gave out choice cuts to the poor, so that no one should be hungry on that happy day.

That was the year when there was trouble along the border. It had been definitely settled that the St. Croix was the boundary line between Maine and New Brunswick, but what happened after you reached the source of the St. Croix? According to treaty, the boundary was to follow vaguely the course of a watershed that, on close inspection, did not seem to be there. So, of course, there was trouble; with twelve thousand square miles known as 'disputed territory', and both countries starting to cut wood on it, and both countries ordering each other off. In those days, and for many years afterwards, the boundary line was referred to as 'The Line'. People spoke of going up or down 'The Line'.

The Governor of Maine wanted to take a bite out of the Madawaska district, which considered itself British. He sent a man named Baker with an American flag and a paper, explaining matters, that the Governor would like the inhabitants to sign; following which indiscretion Mr. Baker spent some time in the Fredericton jail.

Next came word that Mr. Greely, the census-taker from Maine, was over in Madawaska taking the census. Governor Harvey sent word to the Governor of Maine that this was not his job, and Mr. Greely was arrested. Governor Harvey also sent word to Governor Colborne in Quebec that things were looking serious along the border, and Governor Colborne sent down a whole regiment of men and artillery marching into Madawaska. Governor Harvey called out the New Brunswick militia; and Nova Scotia also promised to help. By this time Maine was assembling forces and building fortifications in the Aroostook region. A force of armed wood cutters surprised Mr. McIntire, the head of the American party, and marched him off to Fredericton and a party of Americans seized Mr. McLaughlan, the New Brunswick warden, and marched him off to Bangor, and then the war was on!

It is known as the Aroostook War, where it is known at all. This little war that started in the heart of the timber forests, all about twelve thousand square miles of disputed wilderness, was a great war in its way and it should be mentioned in all history as an example to all other wars. The Aroostook War was remarkable because it was a war where no blood was shed and the issue was settled because two fine military gentlemen, who knew what war meant, were able to see each other's viewpoint and come to a perfect understanding through messages written and exchanged in the most courteous language.

The American government, rather embarrassed by the behaviour of Maine, felt that this was no time to make war on British territory, while Britain was at peace with all the world; and over in London, Lord Melbourne was daily instructing a little blue-eyed queen about her possessions in North America, making it all so interesting with that 'fine soft voice of his'. So the States sent Major-General Winfield Scott to settle the question, and they could not have sent a better man. New Brunswick could not have had a better person than Governor Harvey at the head of affairs, and after several and various courtly interviews, the militia was withdrawn and the King of the Netherlands was asked to decide the question of the boundary line; which he did.

All this time St. Andrews had been watching redcoated soldiers drilling on the Barrack Hill.

Two old letters, directed to the Colonel of Militia at St. Andrews, are of interest in connection with these events. One is from Mr. Nehemiah Marks, of St. Stephen, dated July 14th, 1837:

Dear Sir:

Yours of 12th inst. come to hand, in regard to movements in State of Maine, on the arrest of Greely by our Authority, is not much talked of in this quarter and Calais. The general opinion is that there will be no troops sent on the line without orders from the General Government and that the question of the boundary line will be settled by the General Government. However the State of Maine is getting vesty, it would be well to keep a good look out on their manoeuvres.

I am going to Boston by land next week; if anything turns up in regard to marching of troops on the frontier, I will write you by mail.

There was a great excitement yesterday at Calais; about 40 Indians, or rather white men dressed in Mohawk style, in open daylight took the Custom House officers in Calais, brought them over to Milltown and took them in the woods. Their object was to make them give up the informant of some laths searched a few days since. After keeping them some time they released them. You would have been pleased to have seen the Indians come down in single file, as black as jet, with red shirts; they made a fine appearance.

The Calais guards turned out, but were afraid to go after the Indians; the mob is amongst themselves. This morning the Cutter from Eastport came up, well armed, and what course they will follow, I cannot tell.

Things there looks bad when the Authority cannot be protected. I understand that one of the officers, Mr. Veazey, got a letter yesterday stating if he did not give up the informant, they would burn his house over his head. I am told that his family left their house and all the inhabitants last evening were under arms. This looks like Liberty!

Where is the government like the British? I say, Where? My opinion is that every good subject should hold himself in readiness at a moment's warning to turn out and protect the Province, if required.

In regard to our Battalion of Militia, I would recommend to you to apply for four or five rounds of ball cartridge and have them sent up. We have not any in case of difficulty. I will see that the arms are in good order with good flints, in case they might be wanted. If you cannot get the cartridges from the government, if I could purchase 1000 bullets I would have some cartridge made at my own expense. If you know of any for sale, please let me know. I think it is necessary to have some, if for no other purpose than to keep good order and to strike a terror on a lawless mob.

Should anything turn up worth while I will let you know, as I am going to Boston next Wednesday; and if you think it necessary to purchase some powder there I will do so, if it cannot be got at St. Andrews or St. John at less expense. In turning out at Calais they can hardly get a musket.

Trusting to see you soon, I am, Dear Sir,

Your most Obt. Ser.
NEHEMIAH MARKS.

The second letter is from that delightful person, James Brown, 'The Honourable Jimmy', as he was called. He had come from Scotland, as a boy, to a little rocky farm at Tower Hill, some twenty miles from St. Andrews. There he worked hard all day and studied all evening by the firelight. He could claim relationship to the poet Burns, whose works he could repeat by heart. The fireplace on a rocky farm seems to have been an excellent place to get an education,

106

and the Honourable Jimmy soon found himself seated in the House of Assembly, where his great fund of general knowledge and his poetic instinct gave him a happy command of oratory. He was a tolerant, genial, tactful man, with a great sense of humour and a genius for statesmanship. He greatly loved simplicity and the little rocky farm. Later we hear of him in the Crown Land Office, where he did much for the advancement of the province. Charlotte County was very proud of the Honourable Jimmy. We find this letter from him written to the Colonel of Militia at St. Andrews:

Fredericton.
4th January, 1838.

Dear Colonel:

We have now been a week in session, and although the ordinary business is in progress, our great and pressing object is the defence of the Province, and the assistance of our brethren in the Canadas. A select committee has been raised for the express purpose of devising means to carry that object with effect, and we were a long time in conference with the Commander-in-Chief upon it. This day our plans are agreed upon and we intend to report them to the House tomorrow. We propose immediately to raise two Provincial Battalion (1600 men) to arm and equip and drill them; to be for the time being on the same footing as regular troops.

Expect about 60 volunteers from each militia battalion, and intend to give £4,000 towards the expense.

Despatches were this morning received from Quebec, from which we learn that Col. Booth and the 43rd arrived safely there. We learn also that a considerable rebel force is collected at Navy Island and that, in consequence, two Regiments are ordered from Quebec to Upper Canada. All the available force is in the meantime ordered from these two Provinces to Lower Canada, and the detachment of the 34th now in Fredericton will leave immediately. The Militia will do garrison duty.

The Rebellion appears to be quashed at present but the country is in a very unsettled and precarious condition. We are here however determined to maintain our connexion with the Parent State, and this above all others is the great object of our present legislature.

I called upon and conversed with two gentlemen, before I left St. David, with a view to giving you their names as proper persons for Militia officers in our Company. The first is Mr. John Nesbitt, formerly a soldier in the 74th. He is a decent respectable man of good personal appearance and well-informed. The second is Mr. Justin Moore. He is the son of T. Moore, Esq., and a smart young man. They both promised to attend to their duty should they be appointed.

A number of Petitions and Legislative matters connected with our County have already been before us, but I have not since heard of our proposed amendment to the Militia Law.

I remain Dear Sir,

Your obedient servant,

JAMES BROWN, JUN.

The references in this letter to the sending of troops to the Canadas was for the purpose of quelling a rebellion, chiefly French in origin, that had broken out there. The Navy Island referred to here is an island in the Niagara River. The New Brunswick border was not the only border that was in trouble in those troubled times.

The States refused to accept the boundary that the King of the Netherlands arranged, so the 'Line' remained 'disputed' for another five years.

The Governor of Maine wanted to wait for a while and then take another bite off the corner of Madawaska, as it would be safer not to have troops coming down from Quebec the way they did through that region. So the 'Line' still remained indefinite.

By the year 1842 this 'disputed territory' was getting on everybody's nerves and England sent out Lord Ashburton, who had a consultation on the subject with Daniel Webster; and report says that they spent a most convivial evening together. After which his Lordship was quite willing to accept Webster's point of view, and between them they decided that a few thousand miles of wilderness land were not worth fighting over, and that Maine should be allowed to retain the first bite it had taken out of the Madawaska district, but should not be allowed another mouthful. This, on the whole, was somewhat more favourable than the arrangement made by the King of the Netherlands; but New Brunswick found that first bite Maine had taken out of her well-wooded territory, most inconvenient; and as the militia were very well drilled by now, they would not have minded a little fighting. However, it was a great relief to have the matter settled at last, even if it did leave a somewhat unsatisfactory boundary.

Through all these changing scenes, Mehetible Calef lived on, in the old house near the head of the town where her father had planted the elms. They were grown to enormous trees by now, and Mehetible Calef was an old woman, the last of the Loyalists. She had brought up a family of ten children, the youngest of which had been killed by a falling tree at the age of nine years; another son, Horatio Nelson, had died at sea; and now word came of the death of her daughter, Dorothy, who had married Adam Jack and lived in Saint John. It distressed her greatly not to have been at the bedside of her daughter. She would willingly have walked, she told them, had they but let her know in time. Old as she was, she took the long drive to Saint John to care for her daughter's family.

The story is told that, while driving through the night with her grandson, a boy of seventeen, they were chased by a pack of hungry wolves. The stout old farm horse galloped wildly on and finally brought them safely to Lepreau, where they spent the night, the wolves disappearing at the sight of the light from the houses. That was the old lady's last adventure. She eventually gave up the house by the elms and made her home with her married sons. We find her mentioned in letters of that day, a tranquil figure amid the life of a busy household: "Grandmama is starting the fall knitting," or "Grandmama has a troublesome cough but does not complain," or "Grandmama is dozing by the fire." What were her thoughts as she dozed by the fire? Was she thinking of the little girl who carried a basket of food to a fugitive Captain? Did she hear again the derisive cry of 'Tory'? Was she riding again along that stretch of shore to the rescue of the starving Goldsmith family? What changes she had lived to see! In the year 1860 this courageous old woman died and was buried in the old King Street burying ground where so many worthy old Loyalists are awaiting the final resurrection, as their tombstones tell us.

15 THE COMING OF THE RAILWAY

THE great and absorbing topic of interest in St. Andrews, at this period, was the building of the railway. For years the project of a St. Andrews and Quebec Railway had been talked of. As far back as 1835 application had been made to the House of Assembly for a grant, and a board of directors had been appointed and meetings were held, often at Squire Wilson's at Chamcook. Delegations were sent to England; companies were formed and no stone was left unturned to bring about the great project.

The first committee of management for the Association consisted of Honourable James Allanshaw, Thomas Wyer, Samuel Frye, James McMaster and Adam Jack, Secretary and Treasurer.

We find Squire Wilson sailing over to Ireland after this and visiting Earl FitzWilliam. He returned home with a load of Irish navvies to work on the railroad.

Building a railroad in those days was a tremendous undertaking, and the first plan was to carry it from St. Andrews through to Quebec. The Ashburton Treaty was a great blow to the Association; it meant building many more miles of road, as the route to Quebec would have been much shorter if it could have been taken across the bite that Maine took out of New Brunswick. In fact, the whole subject subsided for a time, and it was not until the year 1852, on the 4th of June, that the great ceremony of turning the first sod took place at Bartlett's Mills. This was made a very grand occasion. Dr. Samuel Frye, who was supervisor of roads at the time, had built a road from the St. John Road at Chamcook through the woods to Bartlett's Mills, near the St. Stephen Road. This road is still known as the Frye Road, and it was through this road that the procession arrived at the spot where Bartlett's Station now stands, about ten miles from St. Andrews.

The procession was composed of all the directors, shareholders, guests and leading citizens in carriages and wagons, the leading carriage bearing the Royal Standard—an immense procession. It left the Court House at half-past nine in the morning, proceeding through Chamcook to the Frye Road.

Colonel Murray, being the Administrator of Justice for the Province at that time, was invited to be present; so he and his lady arrived in their carriage at 12 o'clock, having driven all the way from Fredericton.

Bartlett's Mills was gay with flags and a pavilion or bower had been built where a "cold collation" was served after the ceremony.

To Mrs. Murray was given the honour of raising the first turf, which we are told she did "very gracefully". Parson Alley said a prayer, and then Colonel Hatch made a speech and told them what wonderful things railroads were for developing countries. A salute of nineteen guns was fired and then there were more speeches; His Honour told them how much pleasure it had given himself and Mrs. Murray to assist; and Mr. Brookfield, the contractor, and Mr. Light, the engineer, each made a speech. They then drank "the health of her Majesty" and "success of the undertaking" in most excellent champagne, amid deafening

112

cheers. After the "cold collation" in the bower, they sang "God save the Queen" and drove home tired, but happy.

Never through all its varied career has that railway line, which runs from St. Andrews out past Bartlett's Mills, to McAdam Junction, received so much attention as it did on that June day many years ago, when Mrs. Murray so gracefully lifted the first sod and deposited it in a wheelbarrow.

It has had a precarious career, that little railway. It was called the St. Andrews and Quebec Railway at first, when it was supposed to be heading for Quebec. It was next called the New Brunswick Railway; it was also called other names (not suitable for publication) by some of the shareholders. It eventually ran into Woodstock, and very nearly ran into bankruptcy; and finally in 1887 it reached Quebec and was absorbed into the great C.P.R. System, where it now peacefully remains; but it will never see a ceremony the like of that which celebrated its birth on the 4th of June, 1852, when that multitude assembled in the heart of the wilderness. And what went they out for to see? A little lady, very gracefully placing a lump of sod in a wheelbarrow, a prophet. Oh, more than a prophet! That lump of sod was the symbol of a wondrous future prophesied for them.

The building of the railway brought out several English families, who made their home in St. Andrews and added much to the life and activity of the town.

Mr. Julius Thompson was the first manager of the railway and for him was built that pleasant house

113

beyond the railway station, which has unfortunately been recently demolished.

Mr. Henry Osburn succeeded Mr. Thompson as manager. He married a grand-daughter of Colonel Wyer's and for many years they lived at the lovely old house beyond the railway station. It is only a memory now, but it was like a little bit of England, transplanted beside the cedars and spruces that surrounded the Indian reservation. The old gabled house had deep wainscoted windows that opened on a lovely garden and tennis court shut in by cedar hedges, a garden that was always gay with children and guests and flowers. On the other side were the stables and the kennels with dappled hounds. Mr. Osburn was a keen sportsman and enjoyed going on hunting trips with John Nicholas, the Indian, for his guide.

After the railway passed into the hands of the C.P.R., Mr. Osburn and his family returned to England, where they had inherited an estate near London. Old John Nicholas never forgot them though he lived to be over one hundred years old. He always spoke of Mr. Osburn with deference and respect, though he always called him "Henry." Still at the Indian encampment they will show you quaint old photographs of the Osburn family and tell you stories of the days when they lived at the Point.

Years after Mr. Osburn's death, during the World War, when Mrs. Osburn, then a very old lady, was having tea with her family and some friends in their pretty English drawing-room, an alarmed housemaid appeared saying that some kind of soldier was at the door, who said he was an Indian and insisted on seeing Mrs. Osburn.

One of the company suggested that he should be sent to the kitchen and given something to eat, but the gentle old lady, from her sofa, commanded that he be brought to her. She knew that it must be the son of her husband's old guide and friend, who would bring back to her memories of her old home among the spruce and cedars of her native land. The excited housemaid ushered in a fine-looking young Indian, straight and tall and smart in his khaki uniform, and the best marksman in the British Army.

He entered the room with all the tranquil composure of the pure-bred Indian, and sat beside the sofa and talked to the sweet old lady, answering her many questions. He sat next her at the tea table and entertained the entire company with stories such as they had never heard before. It was as though for that brief hour conditions were reversed and a bit of the Indian reservation at the Point had been transplanted to an English drawing room.

St. Andrews was a very gay and busy place in the early days of the railroad, with a very charming social life. It was still a garrisoned town; also men-of-war frequently visited its harbour. The new English families had to be entertained, and the old Loyalist element loved to dispense a bountiful hospitality. Squire Wilson still kept open house at Chamcook, and Mrs. Wilson still played and sang for them, as gentlemen with lavender gloves and long Dundreary whiskers guided demure ladies in flounces and crinolines through the stately quadrille.

Mr. Light, the young and energetic engineer, who had come to build the railway, proved to be a very fascinating gentleman, and scattered broken hearts along his brilliant pathway, but seems to have escaped himself without matrimonial entanglements. Some of the gentlemen of the town sent him a rather illuminating valentine on the subject, which began:

> O, Mr. Light, you lucky dog
> You set the ladies all agog.

Valentines of a poetical nature were much in vogue in those days.

We hear also of Captain de Whal, of her Majesty's ship *Cordelia* who also had most ingratiating ways with the ladies. When his ship sailed, he presented his photograph to every lady he had met in St. Andrews, and most adroitly made each fair creature think that she was the only woman in the world to receive such a favour. Even to this day there may be found, in the old family albums, the picture of that gallant sailor, looking rather bored with his brass buttons, gold braid and medals.

Archery was a favourite pastime for the ladies; it was a form of sport that crinolines did not render prohibitive. The gentlemen played cricket. Croquet was another popular game. In the evening they played whist, or the ladies worked at their embroidery while one of the gentlemen read aloud.

Dickens was then at the height of his popularity and they used to have Dickens evenings. In the winter there were still those sleighing parties to the Old

Exchange. In the summer they often rode horseback; the ladies with long flowing habits and beaver hats with trailing veils.

A very pleasant, peaceful, decorous age! An age of polite accomplishments, feather beds, flannel petticoats and family parties! An age that was easily shocked, that accepted pleasures warily and mourned prodigiously! An age that appeared ineffectual in the extreme, and yet an age of great achievement, that age that we call Victorian!

Hidden away from these festivities, we find the story of a tragic romance. If you walk up King Street, past the school house towards the big elm, you will find, on your left, a field where lilacs and syringas grow and columbines blossom in the spring. In the early days, it was a well-kept garden; a house stood at the farther corner. It is still known as the old Donaldson place. There, in days gone by, people would sometimes see a young and beautiful lady who came out at twilight and walked up and down the garden walk between the lilacs and syringas. She never appeared in the light of day; she was always alone, no one even spoke to her; she took no part in the festivities that were going on around her; she was a prisoner in her father's house, a disgrace to the family. Those were the days of stern parents and submissive daughters. The story goes that when she was a very young girl, she had married the Admiral on a ship then in port, who was much older than herself and more interested in the affairs of the Navy than in his pretty little bride. He took her back to England, where she found life rather dreary until her husband's young and charming secretary undertook to make things more interesting for her. When they finally discovered they were in love with each other, the secretary, being a noble youth, decided he must resign his position and they parted forever; but, unfortunately, the leave-taking was interrupted by the Admiral, who fell into a towering rage and promptly sent her back to an outraged father in St. Andrews; and so she was kept in solitary disgrace ever after. The Admiral had said that some day he would send a ship to St. Andrews bearing papers of divorce, and so she sat all day at an upper window, looking over towards Clam Cove Head, watching for the ship with the papers of divorce. Only after sunset was she allowed to walk out under the lilacs.

One day, when she had left her watch-tower to get a book in the drawing-room, the maid, not knowing she was there, ushered in a gentleman who had come to see her father. It was Mr. Light; he bustled in with his hands full of papers, anxious to talk with Mr. Donaldson on important business of the railway. The poor lady, however, seeing this strange gentleman with the papers in his hand, took him to be the Admiral's messenger with the divorce. The shock was too great for her heart, that was already broken, and she fell to the floor in a fainting fit from which she never recovered.

There is another story of this period, which is less tragic and more entertaining. It is told of a Lieutenant Quayle, who was stationed at the garrison in St. Andrews at that time. He was a gay and reckless young officer and a great favourite. It happened that a large public ball was given at Eastport and Lieutenant Quayle made one of a party from St. Andrews, which attended. He was much taken with a pretty young Eastport maiden, with whom he danced all evening; and as the wine flowed freely, he was indiscreet enough towards the end of the evening to remove his signet ring and place it upon her finger.

The next day he likewise indiscreetly told of this incident to Sheriff Jones and Mr. Campbell, the postmaster. A few days later he received a soiled and badly written letter from Eastport, that appeared to be from the lady's brother, asking his intentions. As his intentions were certainly not matrimonial, he wrote at once and said so. This brought forth a most indignant letter from the brother, challenging him to a duel if he refused to marry his sister. The distressed Lieutenant consulted the Sheriff and the Postmaster, who agreed that there was no other course than to accept the challenge, and they both agreed to act as seconds and make all arrangements. Deer Island was settled on as the place of meeting and the party went over in a boat, taking Dr. Gove with them as an extra precaution. They decided, if the lady's brother did not turn up within half an hour of the time fixed, that they might safely conclude his courage had deserted him and return home, having valiantly performed their part in the transaction. Much to the satisfaction of poor Lieutenant Quayle, no one appeared, and they had quite a pleasant trip home.

Shortly after this incident, Lieutenant Quayle was removed from the garrison at St. Andrews and his place was filled by Captain Wells, an older and more sedate person.

Later on it happened that both these gentlemen were ordered to the Crimea. One day, at an hotel in Constantinople, where Captain Wells was having breakfast, he heard some other officers talking at a near by table. Hearing St. Andrews mentioned, and also the name Quayle, he joined the group and discovered the same Lieutenant Quayle who had been his predecessor. They exchanged news of St. Andrews and Quayle told him that it was the pleasantest place he had ever been stationed at, except for one unfortunate incident; and he related the details of the duel, and there in that remote foreign city, he learned from Captain Wells that the Sheriff and the Postmaster had written those letters themselves and the irate brother was a myth.

Sheriff Jones lived in the red brick house on King Street next to the Record Office. He brought up a large and interesting family; perhaps the one best remembered in St. Andrews is Mr. Owen Jones, who rose to a position of considerable wealth and prominence in England and made his home in London. He was a very handsome man with a charming personality, but owing to a fatal propensity for nicknames in St. Andrews, he was always called 'Roary' in his youth. Years afterwards, when he returned to his native town, a wealthy gentleman in a top-hat and frock coat, his old friends still welcomed him as 'Roary'; and when he died, he left money to be expended on an iron fence to enclose the old Loyalist graveyard; and to this day the old inhabitants refer to it as 'Roary's' fence.

The Postmaster and his wife were a charming old couple with a delightful sense of humour. Mr. Campbell always disliked to tell people who asked for their mail, that there was nothing for them. When attractive young ladies came to the window and asked for their mail, he would say, "Yes, my dear; yes, my dear", and fumble around the office until he found at least a paper or pamphlet to hand them; but when less interesting people called and there was nothing for them, he would say "Who the deuce would write to you?"

Mr. Campbell was always in his pew on Sunday morning and always took a nap during the sermon. One day, however, a preacher with a very loud voice had come from a neighbouring parish to take the service. His sermon was about the parable of the man without a wedding garment. The preacher thundered his precepts from the pulpit and greatly disturbed the Postmaster's slumbers. Finally, quoting from the parable, he roared out "And he was speechless", at which Mr. Campbell wakened up and remarked "I wish to Heaven you were", loud enough for all the near by pews to hear.

There are amusing stories told of a lady who loved to entertain, but was rather irresponsible as a housekeeper. Her invitations, however, were always accepted with great pleasure because her parties afforded more interest and excitement and were unique in comparison to the rather formal parties held at that time.

It was the day of elaborate suppers, served any time from ten o'clock until midnight. At one of these interesting parties, when the guests were beginning to wonder when refreshments would be served, the hostess returned from the kitchen regions and asked if one of the gentlemen would assist in getting the butter, which was on a shelf in the cellar and the cellar was flooded. An amiable young man volunteered his services for the lady in her dilemma, and the guests later, assembling around the cellar door, watched him by the light of a tallow candle launch himself in a large wooden wash-tub, which he guided with a pole across the watery waste in quest of butter.

The chief domestic of this establishment was a little man named Angelo, who spoke broken English and claimed Malta as his birthplace. He seems to have filled any post from attending to the garden and livestock to taking the children out for an airing.

On one festive occasion, while the guests were all seated primly in the drawing-room which was lighted by two candles on the centre table, Angelo rushed into the room, seized a candle, explained that the pig was dying and rushed out. A malicious gentleman of the party arose and blew out the remaining candle and, in the darkness, loudly kissed the back of his hand, which put all the prim little ladies in a flutter of terror.

Endless stories and anecdotes could be told of the everyday life of this little town. It would seem they never forgot a joke, and tales of both comedy and tragedy have been handed down through generations.

16 THE FENIAN RAID

I N 1866 there was again trouble on the border. That was the year of the Fenian Raid, which caused considerable excitement in the town of St. Andrews.

The American government was not responsible for this trouble. It was an uprising that received its chief incentive from Ireland, which at this time was in an unsettled state and showing a rebellious spirit towards British government. There had been an enormous emigration from Ireland during the time of the potato famine, twenty years before, and many of these Irish people had enlisted in the American Army during the Civil War. When disbanded after the war, they were restless and looking for further excitement and were easily misled by the American idea that the British colonies were slaves to British tyranny, a delusion which even 1812 had not entirely dispelled from the minds of the uneducated and those who lived at a distance from the border. Many native Americans joined the Fenians and were recruited in New York, under their Irish leader, Doran Killian. They were fully persuaded that the British Colonies could easily be roused into a rebellion and that would be a good thing for poor old Ireland in her present frame of mind; and the American recruits thought they would tread the flowery path of glory, leading the Province of New Brunswick, and probably Nova Scotia as well, into the fold of the United States.

Word of this movement came from New York, and recruiting was started all over the Province.

The first instalment of Fenians arrived in Eastport on April 10th, with a schooner laden with arms and munitions.

There was much talk of Confederation going on in the Provinces, and the Fenian leaders held a meeting in Calais to explain to all good American citizens that this should be violently opposed or they would soon have another Empire on their Continent of America.

The American government, during this outbreak, behaved in a very friendly way; they finally sent a force of infantry to prevent the Fenians from crossing the border.

Every day Fenian troops could be seen drilling on the fields near Red Beach and Robbinston.

Fort Tipperary bristled with soldiers. Seven batteries had been sent from St. John and remained in St. Andrews for three months. Three local batteries of artillery were formed with fourteen companies of infantry; and regular troops were sent from Halifax. Besides all these, there were the Home Guards, who met for drill and supplied themselves with a simple uniform consisting of scarlet flannel coats.

A new St. Andrews battery was formed under Captain Henry Osburn, Lieutenant Thomas T. O'Dell and Second Lieutenant Walter B. Morris.

That was the gayest summer ever known in St. Andrews, with the town full of delightful young officers and ships of war patrolling the St. Croix; the element of danger was just enough to be interesting without being alarming. There were many parties and private theatricals.

The Fenians never really had the courage to cross the border. They landed one night on Indian Island and seized the British flag from the customs house; and then up came Captain De Whal in the *Cordelia* and despatched rockets, which was the signal to call out the forces. Captain Osburn's battery answered with the guns from Fort Tipperary and the whole force turned out, enough to frighten any Fenian. The *H.M.S. Duncan* sailed up the St. Croix and fired a few shots just to show what the British Navy could do and that rather upset the companies drilling in the fields on the other side.

Finally, the Fenians got discouraged and went home and the American government seized the schooner load of arms and munitions. The troops gradually dispersed from Fort Tipperary and things were quiet again along the border.

Fifty years later the few surviving veterans, who had nobly defended their country on this occasion, received from the government a medal and a bonus of one hundred dollars.

17   AFTER CONFEDERATION

IT MUST be remembered that all this long while St. Andrews was not in Canada. New Brunswick was a Crown Colony, as were all the other Provinces of British North America. It was only Quebec and Ontario that were known as Upper and Lower Canada.

Each Province was governed by a governor sent out from England, and all the more important problems were decided in London.

For years there had been much talk of uniting the colonies under one government, but it was not until July 1st, 1867, that the Confederation of all the British North American countries took place, with the seat of government at Ottawa, and the Dominion of Canada was created.

St. Andrews then became part of Canada. The town had started in Sunbury County, Nova Scotia, and next was in New Brunswick, and now found itself in Canada without the trouble of moving. The first of July was always kept as a holiday in commemoration of this great event.

A well-known story is told of Sir Leonard Tilley in this connection. When the Fathers of Confederation were discussing the subject of an appropriate name for the confederated provinces and had finally decided on Canada, Sir Leonard said he had read that morning, as was his custom, the portion of scripture appointed for the lessons in the Book of Common Prayer, and had been much struck by the appropriateness of a verse from the prophet Zechariah: "And His dominion shall stretch from sea to sea". He would like, therefore, to suggest that this country be called "The Dominion of Canada"; and that is what it has been called ever since; all because a fine old statesman read his Bible every morning.

Sir Leonard and Lady Tilley are well remembered in St. Andrews. They owned a beautiful house on the hill near the old Donaldson lot and spent many summers there, often seen driving out on fine afternoons in their barouche with liveried coachman.

Sir Charles Tupper, also one of the Fathers of Confederation, lived in St. Andrews. He purchased the old Walton farm and the family remained there for several years. The place was called 'Highland Hill' then, but is now known as 'Clibrig'. Sir Charles Tupper was known as Dr. Tupper at that time, but was afterwards knighted.

The prosperity of St. Andrews was declining at this time. It was no longer a garrisoned town; the British free trade policy had seriously affected its lumber industry. The West Indian trade and ship-building were waning with the introduction of iron ships and steamboats.

The old race of merchant princes had passed on and few had come to take their place.

But it was still a pleasant place to live in, and people who had private means stayed on in the fading shadow of the pomp and elegance of a bygone day. High teas were the favourite form of entertaining, and took the place of the elaborate dinners of the old military days, which were served with a formality that might have graced the dining-table of nobility. In those days servants, well-trained for the officers' mess, would deftly remove the damask tablecloth and place the decanters in coasters on the polished mahogany for the gentlemen, after the ladies withdrew. But that age was passing. High teas were less formal, but quite lavish in their way and very enjoyable; and people liked to live in St. Andrews. The climate was pleasant—so were the people. A peaceful little town, surrounded by hills and sea and memories of a romantic past. No wonder people liked to live there.

Every summer brought more visitors to the town, and the Argyle Hotel was built for their accommodation. It was an extremely ugly building, with its mansard roof and absurd ornamental tower. It stood at the end of the town on low ground, not far from the Marsh. It was considered quite a fine hotel in those days, and many interesting people came to spend their summers there. Mr. Thomas Wheelock's family used to stay at the old Argyle, bringing with them their Chinese servants in gay native dress. Mr. Robert Burdette of Philadelphia, Mr. Robert Gardiner of Boston, and many others, can be remembered who spent their summers at the Argyle Hotel.

That was the age of bustles and fans and draperies and sunflowers and bulrushes and garden parties; an age that cherished the delusion it was aesthetic.

Then came the Land Company, buying up property and making extensive plans for developing the place for a fashionable summer resort, and putting all the peaceful citizens into a flutter, especially those with property to dispose of. Some of the inhabitants were rather skeptical of the scheme, and the following poem was published in the *Bay Pilot*:

1888

The wintry sun at eve went down
Behind the Devil's Head
As Keezer rang the village bell
To show the day was dead.

And every old inhabitant
    As he strolled home to tea
Was conversing with his neighbour
    Of the Boom that was to be.

There was no doubt about it,
    This was no "Argyle Sham",
For companies were forming fast,
    Led on by Mr. Cram;
And capitalists from Boston
    Had said "We'll buy the town",
And millionaires of Calais
    Had planked their money down.

And e'en the nabobs of St. John
    Had done their level best;
They bought up all the land they could,
    And took options on the rest.
And the St. Stephen lumber-kings
    Had also fumed and fussed;
The only trouble seemed to be
    They could not raise the dust!

The fathers of our City
    Had met in the Town Hall,
And listened to some speeches
    That had captured one and all;
What care they then for turnips
    Or how the weirs may fish?
For St. Andrews now was going to boom,
    And what more could they wish?

Down at the Point there'll be a park,
    Where now is brush and brake;
And all the water that we drink
    Will come from Chamcook Lake.
They were told in flowing language
    Of how Chataqua's grown,
How Campobello was no good,
    Bar Harbor's day was done.

They found they'd slept for fifty years,
  But were bound to sleep no more;
And then a leading citizen
  Got up upon the floor;
He said, "Oh kind Americans,
  Our town no more we'll hide,
We'll give you Chamcook mountain
  And we'll throw in the Bayside.
We'll give our Point without a word,
  Your promises are bold;
We are quite sure with men like these
  We never shall be sold."

1898

Again the wintry sun went down
  Behind the Devil's Head;
Again 'Old Keezer' rang the bell
  To show the day was dead.
But now the old inhabitants
  On their way home to tea,
Converse in mournful language
  Of the Boom that was to be.

The cows still roam about our streets,
  Horses and geese as well,
And all the water that we drink
  Still comes from 'Berry's Well';
The good old 'Houghton' goes as fast
  As she did in years gone by;
The same old car is on the road,
  No difference I descry—
In fact I notice nothing new,
  For all things seem the same;
The only difference is, they talk
  Of the Boom that never came.

This poem was signed 'Mabel', and it was accepted
with much favour by the people; only Squire Russell, of
Bayside, said he was very sure they would not give

away the Bayside; and Mr. Keezer objected to being referred to as 'Old Keezer'. The authorship was kept a secret for some time; finally it became known that Mr. Osburn's oldest son, Walter, had written it one evening with some other young people, who were spending the evening at the house.

The first section of the prophecy for 1888 was fulfilled almost to the letter; a park was laid out at Indian Point, but it was not kept up; and now the town water supply actually does come from Chamcook Lake, although as late as 1898 'Berry's Well' was the chief source of supply.

The Land Company bought a good deal of property and built the old Algonquin Hotel, which was a wooden building and a much finer hotel than the Argyle, which shortly afterwards was burnt down.

Later on the railway was sold to the Canadian Pacific, and this Company finally bought out the old Land Company and then St. Andrews became fashionable.

18 IN THIS OUR DAY

AND now in this our day—what have we? Here in this little town, founded after much tribulation and with such loyalty, pride and courage—what have we now? We have very much what they themselves desired, those early loyal exiles—a place of everlasting peace, a harbour of unspoiled beauty under the British flag. St. Andrews never grew to be a city and we ought to be thankful for that. It makes one shudder to think of the delicate beauty of our quiet harbour obscured by warehouses, the grime and smoke of factories, the noise and confusion of congested commerce, subways and street-cars; but of this there is little danger. One frequently hears parents advising their children to leave the town, if they seem to be developing commercial instincts.

So, always, it will be a pleasant place to live in; a haven for those who enjoy beauty and peace and flowers and cool sea air.

It is more beautiful in winter than in summer. Then it is bright blue and white with snow-laden fir trees —a more austere and simple beauty; and, as few people have found this out, it is more peaceful in winter than in summer.

In this our day no Redcoats drill on Barrack Hill. The summer residence of the Shaughnessy family was built upon its ancient site. Old Fort Tipperary is no more, having been torn down and replaced by the new summer residence behind the ramparts. The Honourable Marguerite Shaughnessy now lives at 'Tipperary', and another daughter, the Honourable Mrs. R. M. Redmond owns a permanent residence on King Street.

Sir William Van Horne and his island home are an outstanding memory. When at the height of his career as the gifted and successful president of the Canadian Pacific Railway, he purchased Minister's Island, or rather the greater part of it; all except a portion reserved by the heirs of old Parson Andrews. Here he made his summer home. The house, gardens, stables and windmills suggest the Dutch influence of his ancestry. He built an enormous barn and stocked it with the famous Dutch belted cattle and other pure-bred stock. The farm was the wonder of the community. Beautiful drives and pathways were built throughout the island and, with unstinted generosity were thrown open to the public. In this lovely place called 'Covenhoven' Sir William entertained the leading men of his time.

When the tide was on the bar and the island was cut off from the mainland, which happened twice every day, Sir William revelled in the seclusion which it gave him. He could then uninterruptedly enjoy the many diversions which the island afforded. Lady Van Horne, gentle, sweet and gracious, will long be remembered as the lady of that great house who, with her simple hospitable welcome, made everyone who entered feel at ease.

The Van Horne place will eventually go to a great-granddaughter but in the meantime is rented by Judge M. J. Barry and his sister-in-law Mrs. T. A. Mathis, of Tom's River, New Jersey, the wife of Senator Mathis.

The Algonquin Hotel, enormous, gay, and luxurious, rises above the site of the old parade grounds, which are more like some exotic fashion parade today. At this "lordly pleasure house" both Americans and British meet and forget the past.

Below the hotel, overlooking the sea, is 'Dayspring', the spacious residence of Sir James and Lady Dunn. The house, of Dutch architecture, was built by Mr. and Mrs. L. E. Smoot of Washington. Sir

James is of old New Brunswick stock, and from his house in St. Andrews actively controls the mighty industrial organization centered in the Algoma Steel Corporation. Just below 'Dayspring', Lady Davis lives in a house of more recent vintage.

The old Walton farm has changed hands many times since the early days. It was for some years in the possession of an eccentric gentleman named Mr. James, who built the stone house which still remains. Then came the Tuppers. After that the farm was occupied by Mr. Nathan Blakney, a relative of Sir Charles Tupper. The property was finally sold to Senator Robert McKay of Montreal. The old Scottish senator and his wife delighted in making every possible improvement. They loved the prospect of the far-reaching Bocabec Hills beyond the Narrows, with Kilmarnock Head and Chamcook Mountain in the foreground. After the Senator's death the farm was occupied by a daughter, Mrs. Robert Loring, and is now the summer residence of another daughter, the Honourable Senator Cairine Wilson and Mr. Norman Wilson, of Ottawa.

Mr. Edward Mackay has a beautiful house on the old Tomkins property, formerly the site of 'Rosemount', which was the home of Dr. Neville Parker. The original house was burned many years ago, but was rebuilt on the same site by the late Mr. C. E. Smith of Montreal.

The little stone farmhouse at Bayside, where old "Hurricane Jack" Mowat retired from the sea, is now owned by Mr. Frank Ross of Vancouver, whose herds of Herefords are justly famous. The Ross' Douglas

Lake Ranch in British Columbia is the second largest on the continent with five hundred miles of border fence.

Far back in the early days of the old Argyle Hotel, one recalls Mr. Robert Gardiner, president of the Land Company, who did perhaps more than anyone else to promote the interest of St. Andrews as a summer resort. A grandson, Mr. Robert Gardiner Payne of New York lives at the Anchorage, where the first Mass in St. Andrews was said in 1821.

The stone house at Chamcook, where Squire Wilson and his lady dispensed such royal hospitality, was burned long ago and has been replaced by the house now occupied by the Grimmer family.

The two daughters of the late Mr. David Forgan, Mrs. L. P. Dodge and Mrs. Halstead Freeman both of New York, live now on Joe's Point Road and his son, David, lives in the old house.

Another old house which dates back well before 1885 when it was made over by Mr. J. Emory Hoar is now the pleasant summer home of Mr. C. D. Howe. Situated outside the town proper it is unique with its many gables and its primly clipped hedges.

Many still in St. Andrews will remember Mr. George Hopkins and will have sailed with him about the harbour in his beautiful yacht. The Hopkins cottage was originally built by the artist, Mr. George Innes, and is now the summer home of Mr. Hopkins' daughter, Mrs. Hobart Johnson of Wisconsin.

Dean Sills was another member of the summer colony who seemed more than all others to belong to St. Andrews. In the days of his youth he had been curate of the English Church, and at the same time master of the grammar school. He further linked himself with the place by marrying the daughter of Dr. Ketchum, who was at the time the rector. In his later years Dean Sills purchased the picturesque little cottage formerly owned by the Stone family, and there he returned every summer with his family as long as he lived. The house is now the home of Mr. H. B. Robinson.

Most of the old houses still remain, some of them quite changed with the years and a succession of owners. The Charles Ballantyne's of Montreal now have their permanent home in the renovated Rev. Robert Bowser house, Mrs. F. H. Markey lives in the old Edward Ganong home, and the original Markey house is owned by Mr. Murray Vaughan. Mrs. Vaughan's mother, Mrs. H. W. Pillow lives near by in the former McMaster house once the summer residence of Mr. Percy Cowans of Montreal. The Wheelock house is now owned by Mrs. Robert Struthers; and the McKettrick Jones house is still in the family, the home of Mr. Hugh McKettrick Jones. Dr. Garvin Miller of Montreal lives in the Sir Thomas Tait house. Miss Mona Prentice lives in the original Peacock house on Joe's Point Road.

The house originally owned by the Rev. John Cassils, is now owned by Mrs. George Shuter. Mr. Robert Cockburn is Mr. Cassils' great-grandson and his wife is a descendant of old Dr. McStay. The pleasant old McStay house is still in the possession of the family. The McNichol house beyond the Biological Station is owned by Mrs. A. W. Guiness, and Mrs. Frank Hall lives in the old Charles Everett house which in the early days belonged to the Wilson family. They left it to Miss Lucy Sprague, who for many years kept boarders there. Miss Carol Hibbard and her sister Mrs. Carl Cole live in the old Sheriff Jones home, and the Hathaway house next door to the Redmond's house is the summer home of the Eidlizt's of New York. The Tom O'dell house is owned by Mr. Charles G. Cowan of Ottawa.

Mrs. George Hooper of Montreal, a niece of Miss Roberta MacLaren has the Misses MacLaren home, formerly the residence of Sheriff Stuart. A nephew, the present Lieutenant-Governor of New Brunswick, the Honourable D. L. MacLaren rents one of the Algonquin Cottages every summer. Guy Murchie, who has contributed to the local history in his book *The Sentinel River,* lives on Reed Avenue in a house formerly owned by the estate of Mrs. Edward C. Walker of Walkerville, Ontario. The cottage nearest the hotel is still owned by Miss Beth Smith, of Boston.

The Brian Devlin's of Montreal now have their permanent residence in the G. Horne Russell house, the home of the artist whose beautiful paintings have so truly told the story of our country. Another artist who made his summer home at St. Andrews was Mr. William Hope, who came here as a boy with his parents and eventually built a house on the Bar Road known as the old Grove. His son Charlie Hope lives across the road. Nearer the shore, Mr. Edward Maxwell, the well-known Montreal architect, made his summer home 'Tilletudelum', where his wife still lives.

Among the new houses recently built in the old

town are those belonging to Mr. and Mrs. Blair Gordon and Mr. and Mrs. Harry Thorp of Montreal. Miss Catherine Christie of Toronto spends her summers at her camp on Joe's Point Road, and Mr. Gorham Hubbard of Maryland, formerly a summer resident of Campobello has built in St. Andrews across from Greenock Kirk.

Mr. and Mrs. A. A. McGee of Montreal have a bungalow on Joe's Point Road near their daughter Mrs. W. L. Breeze. Another daughter lives with her author husband, David Walker at 'Glengarry' near the Golf Club. Mrs. Walker's uncle, the late Mr. Norman Guthrie (sometimes known as John Crighton) was one of St. Andrews most understanding interpreters. We find constant reminders throughout all his volumes of the little town where he spent so many summers. Titles such as: *The Harbour of St. Andrews, Through Rose Lane, Sailing Between the Islands into the Bay of Fundy, Bocabec,* and many others.

Back in those days one remembers another old friend; a slight, whimsical man in a light gray suit and straw hat, walking through country lanes and asking school children the names of flowers. Often one met him driving in a buggy with a pleasant old lady, who was his mother. He always had some whimsical question to ask or some unusual demand to make, and back of it all we discovered that he had a wonderful knowledge of English literature. People still exchange anecdotes of his original sayings. Any Harvard student would know him, but not as we knew him in St Andrews. They call him 'Copey' at Harvard, but he was never 'Copey' to us; those who knew him well called him 'Charles', the rest of us called him 'Mr. Copeland'. It would not interest St. Andrews to adopt a nickname it had not originated. We read in the papers last year that Charles Townsend Copeland had died in his ninety-third year.

Always associated with Mr. Copeland will be Mr. Henry Rideout, the author; they were both Harvard men and both natives of Calais. They were often together in St. Andrews in those early days.

But of all those who have made St. Andrews their temporary home, there is one who will ever be remembered. Known the length and breadth of Canada, yet it seems to us we know her best. She knew us all, shouldered our burdens, corrected our mistakes, laughed delightedly at our jokes, enjoyed our gossip, forgave our shortcomings, shared our joys and woes, gave us confidence in ourselves, told us stories of the outside world, stories of the people she had met, the treasures she had collected. Everyone who knew her has some anecdote to tell. Some story of her irrepressible wit, her impulsive generosity, her understanding sympathy, and her unexpected rebukes. Her garden still blooms on the sunny side of the hill. The trees she planted are budding with the spring. 'Pansy Patch' still stands on the hillside, the home of Mr. and Mrs. H. D. Burns, board chairman of the Bank of Nova Scotia. And below the hill, the little town is rich in memory of that free spirit whose earthly name was Kate Reed—the wife of Mr. Hayter Reed, one time Indian Commissioner and later the superintendent of all Canadian Pacific hotels. So we, in this our day, have likewise memories to be told to children by the winter fireside as in the days of old.

This is the end of the story, which is a true story and, to quote the Queen of Sheba, "The half has not been told", for in the sleepy little town under the hill, every one has his own story of early days and it would take many books to contain them all.

The traditions of the elders are not forgotten, and if on some fine August morning the old Loyalists should return, sailing up the harbour in a phantom ship, I dare say they would be well satisfied with the appearance of the town. It would probably annoy them to hear sentimental tourists call it St. Andrews-by-the-Sea, or The Village, but otherwise they would find the same peaceful spot with a harbour of unspoiled beauty under the British flag.

THE END

A LIST OF GRANTEES OF ST. ANDREWS

Jean Adams
Jacob Akehorn
Jacob Akehorn, Jr.
William Anstruther
Andrew Arnold
David Arnot
Edmund Bailey
Samuel Bailey
Nathaniel Bailey

James Banks
John Barber
Joseph Betson
John Bean
William Barnsfair
Joseph Baker
John Batie
Thomas Belle
Moses Bernard
John Bennett

John Bowen
John Boldin
Susannah Boyce
Daniel Brown
John Brown
Thomas Brown
James Brown
Joshua Brown
Richard Braddy

Richard Brady
Benjamin Bradford
Joab Bragg
Benjamin Burgess
Philip Burns
John Calf (Caleff)
Patrick Callaborn
Donald Cameron
John H. Clarn

W. Clapton
Duncan Cameron
Alexander Cameron
Colin Campbell
Archibald Campbell
John Campbell
Colin Campbell, Jr.
Donald Campbell
John Campbell
Duncan Campbell

John Carlow
Martin Carlow
Charles Carrick
Roart Cellars
William Chenay
William Chenay, Jr.
John Clayton
Peter Clinch
Robert Conner

John Conner
John Collins
James Collins
William Cookson
John Crafford
David Craize (Craig)
Robinson Crocker
Silas Cummings
John Curry

Joseph Crookshank
Thomas Days
Charles Darby
Honor Davis
David Daltey
George Dawson
Christopher Derrick
John Dixon
William Dixon
James Douty

Alexander Dobin
Jon Dowling
Edward Dogherty
John Dogget
Thomas Dodd
John Dunbarr
John Dunn
Charles Dupnack
David Eastman

Rebeccah Eldridge
Hugh Ellis
Joseph Ellison
Thomas Emerson
James Ferran
Peter Ferdinand
Alexander Ferguson
John Fisher
Richard Fleming

David Fogo
Josiah Fowler
John Fraser
William Gammon
William Gammon, Jr.
William Gallop
Moses Gerrish
Edward Gillinore
John Gilis
Daniel Grant

Hugh Grant
William Grant
Alexander MacNevin
James McNabb
Evan MacPherson
Hugh McPhales
Duncan McVicker
James McVean
John Nason

Joseph Nash
William Nial
James Nicholson
Francis Norwood
Gustavus Norwood
James Norwood
Jonathan Norwood
Jonathan Norwood, Jr.
Samuel Norwood

Samuel Osburne
John Pagan
Robert Pagan
Robert Pagan, Jr.
William Pagan
Thomas Pagan
Joseph Paddock
Archibald Patterson
Thos. Patterson
Tabitha Parsons

Andrew Pattin
William Patten
James Percy
Andrew Peters
Benjamin Pepper
Nathan Philips
Thomas Philips
James Philips
Hybecker Pine

Benjamin Pomeroy
Richard Pomeroy
Miles Post
Dennis Post
Jeremiah Pote
Avis Preble
John Priest
Daniel Ray
William Readhead

Jonathan Rementon
John Rigby
Hyronimus Riter
Edward Ross
Daniel Ross
Henry Ross
John Ross
Thomas Ross
Timothy Roax
John Roax

Alexander Robinson
John Robinson
Michael Ryan
James Russell
Stephen Roberts
Maurice Salt
Matthew Scallion
James Scott, Jr.
John Scott

James Scott
Thomas Grace
John Gray
Jonathan Greenlow
Ebenezer Greenlow
Alexander Greenlow
James Griffison
George Gunn
William George

John Hall
Thomas Haley
Nathaniel Haley
James Hamilton
Robert Hamilton
James Hammon
Zebedee Hammon
Martin Haymas
Hugh Henderson
John Hervey

Maurice Hinley
Amos Hitchings
Ludovick Hildebron
David Hill
Frederick Horn
William Holmes
Esther Ingerson
William Jackson
George Johnson

James Joice
John Jones
Samuel Kelly
William Kelly
Sarah Kenney
James Kervin
John Lay
Hugh Lammey
Daniel Leaman

Mark Linisdon
George Lights
William Linsey
Hugh Linsey
Matthew Limeburner
Peter Littlejohn
Thomas Littlejohn
Ebenezer Linkliter
John Lillie
Zebedee Linnikin

William Lowther
Thomas Mackay
Richard Maher
Nehemial Marks
Silas Mawby
Andrew Martin
John Matherson
James Melaney
John Meloney

William Merchie
Benjamin Milliken
Benjamin Milliken, Jr.
Thomas Mitchell
Charles Morris, Jr.
Thomas Morris
Robert Merril
Alexander Morrison
William Morrison

William Morris
Sarah Montgomery
David Mowatt
William Moore
Archibald Merphy
Finley Mulcman
Robert Muncur
David McAllew
David McAchrow
Alexander McBean

Neal MacBean
Donald McLean
Peter McCollin
Humphrey McCollin
Laughlin McCurdy
Neal McCurdy
Roderick MacClellan
Alexander McLeod
Hugh McLeod

William McCluskey
Robert McCarter
Angus McDonald
Joseph McDonald
John McDugal
Peter McDirmurd
John McElreah
Duncan McFarlane
John McFale

John McGear
John McIntosh
John McIntire
Duncan McIntire
Lochlan McKinnie
Donald McKinzie
Daniel McLaughlin
Alexander McMullin
Alexander McLean
Robert McLellis

Daniel McMasters
John McNichol
John Shaw
Samuel Sheppard
Joseph Sheppard
David Shields
John Shields
John Sighensparker
James Simmons

Robert Simms
Michael Simpson
William Skelton
John Smyth
James Smith
Joseph Smith
John A. Sowers
William Spencer
Samuel Spencer

Hugh Stewart
Duncan Stewart
Stinson Stewart
Charles Stewart
Allen Stuart
William Stuart
James Stuart
William Stuart
James Stinson
Balshazer Stilkey

William Stevens
William Swaine
Bryan Sweeney
John Symons
Ralph Taylor
John Taylor
Gillam Taylor
James Thompson
Dugal Thompson

Matthew Thornton
Francis Tipping
Thomas Tompkins
William Towers
John Trot
Samuel Trot
James Turner
Nicholas Turner
Thomas Turner
William Turner

Samuel Turner
Peter Vallet
William Vance
Robert Varden
John Wall
James Waller
James Wardwell
Susannah Webb
Francis Welsh

Thomas Wier
Archibald Willison
George Wilie
Thomas Wilson
Matthew Wingood
George Wisely
David Wyer
John Yearston
Jacob Young
James Young